DR CAMPBELL'S *DIARY*

Rev. Thomas Campbell, LL.D.

Rector of Gallown.
Chancellor of Clogher.

Obit June 20th 1795.

Dr CAMPBELL'S
DIARY

OF A

Visit to *England*

IN 1775

Newly edited from the MS. by

JAMES L. CLIFFORD

With an Introduction by

S. C. ROBERTS

CAMBRIDGE

at the University Press

1947

CAMBRIDGE UNIVERSITY PRESS
Cambridge, New York, Melbourne, Madrid, Cape Town, Singapore,
São Paulo, Delhi, Dubai, Tokyo, Mexico City

Cambridge University Press
The Edinburgh Building, Cambridge CB2 8RU, UK

Published in the United States of America by
Cambridge University Press, New York

www.cambridge.org
Information on this title: www.cambridge.org/9780521166348

First published 1947
First paperback edition 2010

A catalogue record for this publication is available from the British Library

ISBN 978-0-521-16634-8 Paperback

CONTENTS

ILLUSTRATIONS

EDITOR'S
ACKNOWLEDGEMENTS

My principal obligations are to Mr S.C. Roberts and Miss Ida E. Leeson, Librarian of the Mitchell Library, Sydney. Without their generous aid, the nature of which will be obvious to readers of Mr Roberts's Introduction, this edition could never have been completed. Thanks are also due to Lieut.-Col. Ralph Isham, the Viking Press and Messrs Heinemann for permission to quote from the *Boswell Papers*; and to Mrs E.B. Scott, a descendant of the Campbell family, for the portrait used as a frontispiece. Professor Frederick A. Pottle has without stint given valuable suggestions and I am especially grateful to Mr Harold Williams for providing the material for Note 141. The following have given help in various ways: Dr R.W. Chapman, Professor E.V.K. Dobbie, Professor Howard Dunbar, Professor J.W. Krutch, Chancellor J.B. Leslie, Mr R.B. McDowell, Mr E.G. Millar, Professor B.C. Nangle, Professor D. Nichol Smith, Mr J.M. Osborn, Dr L.F. Powell, the Hon. John Robb, Professor George Sherburn, Miss Elizabeth Steere, the Rev. Canon T.E. Swanzy. For long hours in puzzling over Campbell's sometimes baffling handwriting, my deep appreciation to my wife.

J. L. C.

COLUMBIA UNIVERSITY
August 1946

INTRODUCTION

On 5 April 1775 Johnson and Boswell were guests of the Dillys at dinner. Boswell took with him an Irish clergyman, Dr Thomas Campbell, who was said to have come to England 'chiefly with a view to see Dr Johnson, for whom he entertained the highest veneration'. Campbell had, in fact, already met Johnson at the Thrales' and was to meet him again on several occasions. Like Boswell, he kept a journal; but, unlike Boswell, he had no vision of himself as a Johnsonian chronicler. In a small pocket-book he made notes of his visits to London, Paris, and Brighton, the greater part of them being devoted to the period 23 February—9 May 1775. These notes were unknown to the world until in 1854 there was published in Sydney the *Diary of a Visit to England in 1775, by an Irishman (the Reverend Doctor Thomas Campbell, author of 'A Philosophical Survey of the South of Ireland') and other papers by the same hand. With notes by Samuel Raymond, M.A., Prothonotary of the Supreme Court of New South Wales.*[1]

In his Preface the editor explained that the manuscript had been found in the offices of the Supreme Court at Sydney, but that he had no knowledge of how it had come there. Of the imperfections of his editing he was fully aware; but of the authenticity of the *Diary* he had no doubt. Whether copies of the book reached England

---

[1] There were two issues of the book. The first bore the imprint on the title-page, SYDNEY: PRINTED BY DANIEL LOVETT WELCH, ATLAS OFFICE; the second, SYDNEY: WAUGH AND COX, BOOKSELLERS AND PUBLISHERS, 111, GEORGE STREET. Some copies of the second issue also contained a page of ERRATA AND ADDENDA.

Introduction

through the ordinary channels of trade is uncertain, but on 21 May 1859 Macaulay wrote in his Diary:

A letter from Sydney with a curious little pamphlet printed there—a *Diary* of Dr T. Campbell, mentioned in Boswell's *Life of Johnson*. The *Diary* contains an account of what the Dr saw during a visit to England in 1775. It by no means gives the notion of a blind fanatical worshipper of Johnson, as I had supposed Campbell to be from Boswell's narrative. There are some odd things as coming from a clergyman; and some passages still more indecorous have been omitted. I observe that Johnson could swear and swear even before a parson when in a passion. The history of the *Diary* is curious. Mr Raymond, Prothonotary of the Supreme Court of N.S.Wales found the MS. behind an old press in his office. Nobody knew how it came there, or could guess. That it is genuine is quite certain. The internal evidence is more than sufficient. I looked into Nichols's *Illustrations of Literary History* and found that Campbell's eldest nephew went in 1810 to Sydney with letters of recommendation to Governor Macquarrie. As Campbell left no children, this nephew no doubt had his papers and took them to New South Wales. Answered Mr Raymond and told him what I had discovered.[1]

From this last sentence it seems clear that Macaulay had received his copy of the *Diary* direct from Samuel Raymond, the editor. It is also clear that he spoke of the book to his friends, among them Henry Reeve, editor of *The Edinburgh Review*. On 1 June he noted in his Diary:

Reeves [*sic*] wants me to review T. Campbell's *Diary*. I will do no such thing. He may, if he likes.

But in a letter to Reeve, written on the same day, he was more conciliatory:

[1] The extracts from Macaulay's Diary, now in the library of Trinity College, Cambridge, are quoted by kind permission of the Master and Fellows.

Introduction

Before you determine anything about Dr T. Campbell's *Diary*, you had better read it. I have lent my copy, which is probably the only copy in England, and do not expect to get it back until next week. When it comes, I will send it to you, and we will then talk further.[1]

Macaulay read the *Diary* again on 12 June and on the 27th wrote to Reeve:

If I were to renew my connexion with the *Edinburgh Review* after an interval of fifteen years, I should wish my first article to be rather more striking than an article on Campbell's *Diary* can easily be. You will, no doubt, do the thing as well as it can be done.

The *Diary*, after all, was small beer; Macaulay had been a giant amongst *Edinburgh* reviewers and he was now a sick man. Nevertheless, his interest in the little book was keen (had not Raymond convicted Croker of yet another blunder?)[2] and the article which appeared in the *Review* for October 1859, written no doubt by Henry Reeve, was based upon the material Macaulay had supplied. It was an article of considerable length—longer, in fact, than the review of *The Virginians* in the same number—and surveyed the *Diary* in detail, with liberal quotations. It also contained a summary of what is recorded of Campbell in the seventh volume of Nichols's *Literary Illustrations*; the Percy-Campbell correspondence in that volume providing the clue, as Macaulay had

[1] For this and the following letters, see J. K. Laughton, *Memoirs of Henry Reeve* (1898), II, 31–6. Macaulay was wrong in regarding his copy as unique. A copy was given to the Athenaeum by A.T. Holroyd on 21 May 1855.
[2] Both Croker in his edition of Boswell and Forster in his *Life of Goldsmith* had followed Nichols in identifying Campbell with the flashy Irishman of Mrs Thrale's letter to Johnson of 16 May 1776.

noted, to the connection between Campbell and New South Wales. For Thomas Campbell had had a nephew, John Thomas, about whom his younger brother, Charles, had written to Percy in 1810 that he was 'just embarking from the Cape of Good Hope...for New South Wales, with strong recommendation to Colonel Macquarrie, who is the Governor of that settlement'.

'We hope', wrote the reviewer, 'to ascertain that this gentleman afterwards held some office in the Supreme Court', and in conclusion:

Dr Campbell's diary has been walled up behind that ancient press in the Supreme Court at Sydney, until, like a pipe of Madeira laid in on the birth of an heir and forgotten on his majority, it has acquired the flavour of a curious liqueur. The world is extremely indebted to Mr Raymond for having brought this document to light; and in any future edition of the *Life of Johnson*, Dr Campbell's notes cannot fail to be inserted.

That paragraph, if not actually written by Macaulay, has acquired the flavour of a curious distillation of Macaulay's style.

The first of the reviewer's hopes was quickly fulfilled and again with the aid of Macaulay, who wrote to Reeve on 11 November:

I have just received the enclosed letter which may, perhaps, interest you. It might be worth while to put a short note at the end of the next number of the *Edinburgh Review*.

It was Macaulay's last communication to the *Edinburgh*. He died on 28 December, and at the end of the January number there appeared, following a tribute to Macaulay, the following note:

Since the publication of our last Number we have received from the Editor of Dr Campbell's Diary, who resides at Sydney, some further particulars which complete the identification of

Introduction

the nephew of Dr Campbell as the person by whom the Manuscript Diary was conveyed to New South Wales.... Mr Raymond now informs us that he had previously ascertained that the Diary had been in the possession of John Thomas Campbell, brother of the Rev. Charles Campbell of Newry. This gentleman was Provost Marshal and for some time Colonial Secretary at Sydney. He died in 1829, and it appears from his will registered in the Supreme Court of New South Wales, that he bequeathed a considerable property to his sisters resident in Ireland. These facts complete the explanation of the singular removal of the Manuscript Diary from Ireland to the place where it was discovered at the Antipodes. It will be interesting to our readers to know that the materials for the article on Dr Campbell's Diary were communicated to us by Lord Macaulay, and that this very note was, in fact, his last contribution to these pages, made within a short time of his death.

It is curious that this explanation seems not to have been noticed by later editors of Boswell. Alexander Napier gives a good account of Thomas Campbell in an appendix to his second volume, but attributes the completed identification of the nephew, John Thomas, to an industrious reviewer in the *Sydney Morning Herald*.[1] In the supplementary volume of *Johnsoniana*, edited by Mrs Robina Napier, Campbell's *Diary* was for the first time reprinted, though not in its entirety; there were some passages which, even in Raymond's bowdlerised version, offended the good taste of 1884.

Birkbeck Hill approached the *Diary* with less enthusiasm. In 1882, when his proposal for a new edition of Boswell was first submitted to the Delegates of the Clarendon Press, Benjamin Jowett had written:

There is also a book about Johnson published by a Dr Campbell, or rather professing to be written by him and pub-

[1] *Life of Johnson*, ed. Napier (1884), ii, 551.

Introduction

lished about 30 years ago in N.S. Wales. It contains accounts of Conversations with Johnson—which I believe to be forgeries, though I remember Lord Macaulay reproving me for doubting them.[1]

Birkbeck Hill himself accepted, with some reluctance, the genuineness of the *Diary* and printed extracts from it in his *Johnsonian Miscellanies*; but he regarded Macaulay's enthusiasm as excessive and, in particular, could not believe that Johnson could ever have said 'Damn the rascal'. If he could have seen the full text of the passage, he would no doubt have dismissed the *Diary in toto*.[2]

Some years ago, having with difficulty obtained a copy of the original edition of the *Diary*, I had a mind to re-edit it on the basis of Raymond's text. But an examination of the text made it clear that a new edition would be worth while only if it could be based on the original manuscript, and the chances of recovering the manuscript seemed remote indeed. But the resolution of Mr Clifford, with whom I discussed the project, was of sterner quality. Undaunted by preliminary discouragement, he persisted in his inquiries and in July 1934 Miss Ida E. Leeson, librarian of the Mitchell Library, Sydney, wrote to inform him that she had found the original *Diary*. The manuscript had not wandered; it had been given to the Australian Library, the forerunner of the Public Library of New South Wales, by Raymond in 1854 and had remained uncatalogued for many years. Photostats were made in due course and thus Mr Clifford has been enabled to present for the first time a complete and accurate text of Campbell's narrative.

[1] Birbeck Hill, *Talks about Autographs* (1896), pp. 49–53.
[2] *Life of Johnson*, ed. Powell-Hill (1934), II, 338, 518.

Introduction

Perhaps it would be more accurate to refer to Campbell's 'notes' rather than to his 'narrative'. Clearly, what he has left is his day-to-day impression of England and the English, hastily recorded and lacking the polish of a finished composition. Jowett mistrusted the record because it 'agreed too much with Boswell'. Similarity to Boswell would surely be as valid an argument for authenticity as for plagiarism; but, in fact, Campbell's record bears no striking resemblance in detail either to the text of Boswell's own Journal or to that of the *Life*.

About Johnson, Campbell is frank enough. He had heard of his prejudices and mannerisms and, when the first meeting took place, he was on the look-out for them. He was not disappointed. One of the less palatable references to Johnson occurs in the account of the dinner at the Thrales' on 1 April 1775. Readers who have had access to the *Private Papers of James Boswell* are of course already familiar with the unfamiliar bawdiness of the anecdotes and the fact that they are reported by both diarists points not to their authenticity but to the probability that they were common tittle-tattle amongst certain members of Johnson's circle.[1]

But Campbell was more than a sightseer or a collector of gossip. He wanted to hear Johnson talk and, in particular, to hear his views about Ireland. The conversation on this topic is duly recorded under the date 11 June 1781, but a fuller account is included in the *Sketch of the Constitution ... of Ireland* appended to Campbell's *Strictures on the...History of Ireland*[2] and it was

[1] See pp. 68–9 and Mr Clifford's note 114.
[2] *Life of Johnson*, ed. Napier, ii, 546–51.

Introduction

characteristic of Johnson that, after a violent explosion against the rebellious Irish, he should conclude by saying:

> Why, Sir, I don't know but I might have acted as you did, had I been an Irishman, but I speak as an Englishman.

Johnson apart, Campbell was an interested, and interesting, observer of English men and manners and especially of English players and preachers.

Few manuscripts have had a more curious history than Campbell's. Laid down in obscurity for half a century, it was brought to light by Raymond. Macaulay stamped it with a vintage character, but other connoisseurs in Johnsoniana were less confident. Now, thanks to Mr Clifford's assiduity, the old wine has been re-discovered. It deserves its new bottling.

S. C. R.

DOCTOR THOMAS CAMPBELL

1733–1795

THOMAS CAMPBELL, the man who kept the Diary, requires some description. To most Johnsonians he is at best a shadowy figure—merely a name appearing several times in Boswell's *Life*—but at the time of his first visit to London in 1775 the tall, handsome Irishman was no shadow. Conspicuously large and stout, with a ruddy complexion, he was always ready to joke about his size. Mrs Thrale tells that once they all laughed when Campbell, speaking to Dr Johnson about another large man ('Bruce of Abyssinia I believe'), had insisted 'indeed now Sir & upon my honour—I am but a *Twitter* to him'.[1] He had an Irish wit, as well as a northern brogue, an ever-present curiosity, and an engaging manner. As Mrs Thrale put it: 'He was a fine showy talking man. Johnson liked him of all things in a year or two.'[2]

Apparently, what impressed people most about Campbell was his agreeable manner. To be sure, Boswell found the visitor almost too affable, and wrote in his

[1] Lansdowne MSS. at Bowood. Mrs Piozzi to Hester Maria Thrale, 23 April 1796. Mrs Piozzi tells the same story in a number of places. See the 1788 edition of Johnson's *Letters* (I, 329); and *Autobiography of Mrs Piozzi*, ed. Hayward, 2nd ed. 1861, I, 99.
[2] *Autobiography, loc. cit.*

Dr Thomas Campbell

Journal on 5 April 1775 of a conversation that day with Mrs Thrale:

I told her that I had asked Dr. Campbell, the irish Clergy-man, to dine today at Dilly's, as he was so desireous to see Mr. Johnson, was so goodhumoured a man, and so thankful for any civilities. That he was quite like a *pet* sheep, (Mrs. Thrale gave me the english phrase, a *cayed* sheep,) went with the cows, walked about the house, and every body, even the children, gave him clover or a handful of corn or a piece of bread out of their pockets. Every body gave something to Campbell —'Poor Campbell'. She thought my idea a very good one.[1]

Of Thomas Campbell's early life we know very little. Born on 4 May 1733 at Glack in the county of Tyrone, he was the eldest son of the Rev. Moses Campbell, curate to the Archdeacon of Armagh, and afterwards rector of the parish of Killeshill.[2] His mother, Elizabeth Johnston, of Tully, county Monaghan, seems to have been of a fairly well-to-do and prominent family. One of her brothers, George Johnston, was M.P. for Portarlington, 1727–30, and another, Baptist Johnston, was M.P. for Monaghan Borough, 1747–53, and High Sheriff of that county in 1728.[3]

Nothing is known of the boy's early schooling, except that he was prepared for college by a private tutor, and entered Trinity College on 15 April 1752, giving his age

[1] *Boswell Papers*, x, 187 (Wednesday, 5 April 1775). The usual spelling of the word used by Mrs Thrale is 'cade'.

[2] See Charles Campbell's letter to Bishop Percy, 28 Feb. 1810. (Nichols' *Literary Illustrations*, vii, 796.)

[3] H. B. Swanzy, *The Vicars of Newry*, Belfast, 1927, p. 16. Campbell's mother evidently had inherited some property. See D. A. Chart, *The Drennan Letters* (Belfast, 1931), p. 22.

Dr Thomas Campbell

as sixteen.[1] Campbell was admitted as a Pensioner—
that is, an ordinary fee-paying student. Two years later,
after an examination, which probably covered 'most of
the Latin and Greek authors of note', he became a
'scholar'.[2]

Having proceeded to the degree of B.A. in 1756
and to that of M.A. in 1761, he was in the latter year
ordained to the curacy of Clogher.[3] For eleven years
after his ordination Campbell performed the duties of
a country curate, enlivened by occasional long visits to
Dublin and the surrounding country. All this time
his two most absorbing interests—research into Irish
antiquity, and the study of pulpit oratory—were being
formed.

Whether Campbell ever married is uncertain. No
definite records are available, and he himself never mentions a wife in any of his letters or his *Diary*. Furthermore, years later J.B. Nichols wrote: 'It is believed that
he was never married.'[4] On the other hand, twentieth-
century descendants of the Campbell family bear witness
to a marriage and actually give the lady's name—Jane

---

[1] Burtchaell and Sadleir, *Alumni Dublinenses*. If the date of his
birth is correct as given by his nephew Charles, Campbell must
have been at least eighteen.

[2] In Trinity College there were seventy scholars, who with the
Fellows formed the corporation. A scholar was exempted from
college fees, held rooms at half rent, had a small salary per annum
and free commons. For a description of student life see also A.P.I.
Samuels, *Early Life and Correspondence of Edmund Burke* (Cambridge, 1923).

[3] J.B. Leslie, *Clogher Clergy and Parishes*, Enniskillen, 1929, p. 62.
Campbell was ordained priest 4 Sept. 1763.

[4] *Illustrations*, VII, 766. Campbell 'had a niece living with him in
1791'.

Dr Thomas Campbell

Holmes of Moyare, Pomeroy Parish.[1] In any event, Mrs Campbell certainly was not alive as late as 1775.

At the death of his father on 26 January 1772, Thomas Campbell, as the eldest son, inherited half the family plate and a lease in Bohard.[2] In the spring of the same year he received from his old college the degrees of LL.B. and LL.D.;[3] and with this recognition came preferment in the church. On 15 August he was collated prebendary of Tighallon, and on 8 February 1773 was made Chancellor of St Macartin's, Clogher.[4]

By the winter of 1775 Dr Campbell was an important church dignitary, a preacher of high repute, and a rising young Irish antiquary. Armed with a little note-book he set out to see something of London and the world; and on 23 February 1775 went aboard the packet boat for Holyhead.

In the account of his journey and his impressions of places and people Campbell was no dry-as-dust recorder. Seldom curbing his naturally acid pen, he gave full vent to his disgust when conditions annoyed him. But he was just as eager to give praise where it was deserved. The

[1] J.B. Leslie, *Clogher Clergy*, p. 62. Chancellor Leslie tells me that he secured the information about the marriage from the late Dean of Dromore, the Very Rev. Henry Swanzy.

[2] J.B. Leslie, *Armagh Clergy and Parishes*, Dundalk, 1911, p. 331.

[3] For the date of the degrees see *Alumni Dublinenses*, p. 130. The two degrees were often conferred simultaneously, and were given at fixed periods after the B.A. on the payment of certain fees and the performance of formal academic exercises. See *Translation of the Charter and Statutes of Trinity College, Dublin*, Dublin, 1749, p. 161.

[4] H. Cotton, *Fastae Ecclesiae Hibernicae*, 1849, III, 96, 104. See also Leslie, *Clogher Clergy*, pp. 62, 87, 152–3. In Campbell's time the parishes of Currin and Killeevan formed the rectory of Galloon, which was the corps of the Chancellorship.

preachers in London, in general, he judged very wooden, and many of the services inferior. An ardent devotee of the theatre, he found many of the London actors unable to approach his own Dublin favourites. On the other hand, there were some for whom he could not withhold the highest praise. Music did not interest him, but painting was one of his hobbies, and he visited all the galleries of prints and pictures. But people interested him most; and since Campbell had some of the recording instincts of James Boswell, it is the accounts of people which make his *Diary* valuable.

The first few men he met in London, as might have been expected, were Irish. But Campbell was not satisfied with seeing the sights of the Capital and dining with his former friends in college; the men and women he wanted to meet were the figures of importance in the intellectual world. The longest entries in the *Diary* describe his days with Dr Johnson and his circle.

How Campbell secured an introduction to the Thrales we may never know, though possibly it was through some Irish business acquaintance. At any rate, on 14 March he crossed the river to Southwark, where he was amazed at the immensity of the brewery, and pleased at the learning of his hostess. That day Dr Johnson was not there; two days later, however, when Campbell dined again with the Thrales, he met the Doctor, as well as the Italian scholar, Baretti. His first impression of Johnson was extremely unfavourable, but fortunately this distaste did not keep him from devoting many pages in his *Diary* to Johnson's conversation.

Boswell is responsible for the story that one of the chief reasons for Campbell's journey this year was to see the great lexicographer. On 6 April 1775 Boswell recorded:

> I mentioned that Dr. Thomas Campbell had come from Ireland to London, principally to see Dr. Johnson. He seemed angry at this observation. DAVIES. 'Why, you know, Sir, there came a man from Spain to see Livy; and Corelli came to England to see Purcell, and, when he heard he was dead, went directly back again to Italy.' JOHNSON. 'I should not have wished to be dead to disappoint Campbell, had he been so foolish as you represent him; but I should have wished to have been a hundred miles off.' This was apparently perverse; and I do believe it was not his real way of thinking: he could not but like a man who came so far to see him. He laughed with some complacency, when I told him Campbell's odd expression to me concerning him: 'That having seen such a man, was a thing to talk of a century hence,'—as if he could live so long.[1]

One of Campbell's most winning traits was his desire to please. On 20 April, when at the Thrales', he heard his hostess tell of her difficulty in getting the son of a poor riding master in the Borough admitted to Christ's Hospital, the famous Blue Coat School. The chief obstacle, it appeared, was that since the boy had been born in Ireland, the necessary papers about his birth were not available. At once Campbell offered to search out the baptismal record and send back a copy.[2]

In London Campbell was struck by the general ignorance about Ireland. Few Englishmen knew anything of their neighbouring island, and scarcely any seemed disturbed by this lack of knowledge. Thence sprang the idea that he might write a book describing the

[1] *Life*, II, 342–3, 519. Also p. 339. Dr Burney insisted that Corelli was never in England.
[2] *Thraliana*, ed. Balderston, I, 118.

Dr Thomas Campbell

historical monuments of Ireland, the places of interest to
tourists, the characteristics of the inhabitants, as they
might appear to a cultivated English traveller. By this
means, as Campbell later described his purpose, he might
'recommend toleration in Ireland, and a more liberal
communication of commercial and political privileges in
England'.[1] If written in 'a light, airy manner', such
errors as were sure to creep in might be considered 'more
venial', and the whole would provide pleasant reading as
well as instruction.

With all this in his mind, Campbell returned to his
home in May 1775. Two months later he set out for
Dublin to gather material for his book. As he planned
it, the work was to be a series of letters, written by
an anonymous Englishman to his friend, John Watkinson, M.D.—the letters themselves to be filled with
sketches of the social life, the local traditions, the historical background of the country through which he
travelled. Like Johnson's *Journey to the Western Islands*
Campbell's book was to be a common-sense account of
a part of the British Isles rarely visited by cultured
travellers.

Campbell remained in Dublin for about a month,
commenting on the buildings, the art, the fashions, the
drinking, and pointing out the obvious comparisons with
London. Dublin, he insisted, was a more hospitable city,
but, of course, visitors were more rare. On the other
hand, Dublin's streets were dirtier and less attractive.

In London, one can rarely want amusement, the very streets
are an inexhaustible source of it. There is something refreshing
in that variety of cheerful objects, which they perpetually ex-

[1] *Illustrations*, VII, 800.

7

hibit. There is such a cleanness in the streets, such a richness in the shops, such a bustle of business, such a sleekness of plenty, such a face of content, and withal, such an air of pleasure, as infuse the most delicious sympathies. Here, we see but little to cheer, or exhilarate reflection, but much to sadden and depress the spirits. There is, indeed, a motion, but it is such, as when the pulse of life begins to stagnate, or like that of the wheel of some great machine, just after the power which impelled it, ceases to act.[1]

After some short jaunts outside Dublin, Campbell on 21 August set out for Kildare—to begin his longer tour. He thus described what he intended to do:

I purpose giving you sketches of the country through which I travel, that you may have some idea of its present state, whether natural or improved. But lest they should seem overcharged with still life, I shall heighten the prospect with human figures as they present themselves; and to vary the scenery, retrospective views of manners, customs, and arts shall be interspersed.

You are not to expect either order or method in the arrangement of my observations: I shall set them down as they occur, without much attention to time, place, or other accident. All I shall promise is, fidelity in reporting facts. . . .

My object is not only to see the face of the country, and learn its present state, but also to compare this state, with what it has been, and what it might be.

And so he began by calling Kildare 'but a poor town', discussing the local antiquities, tossing out compliments for the Irish antiquary, Major Vallancey, and describing his feelings on his recent visit to Shakespeare's birthplace at Stratford. It was all very casual and offhand. From a disquisition on ancient Irish history he shifted

[1] *Philosophical Survey*, pp. 30–1. The following quotations are all from the London edition of this work.

Dr Thomas Campbell

without difficulty to the Ossianic controversy of the moment. Fresh from the London battles of Johnson and the Scotch, Campbell was full of the question and spent twelve pages proving, as all good Irishmen had always known, that Macpherson's versions were forgeries.

For the next two and a half months Campbell wandered in a leisurely manner around southern Ireland, visiting most of the places of interest. At Cashel he astonished the natives by taking measurements of the old ruins, and was astonished himself at the gaiety and high spirits of the gentry, gathered together for a horse-race and an assembly. The ladies he found 'elegantly dressed, in the *ton* of a winter or two since in London', while they seemed to vie with the men in vivacity and 'display of animal powers'. The lot of the common people, on the other hand, he found 'beastly'.

It must not be thought that Campbell's emphasis was solely on local customs. Ingenuously he passed from one idea to the next—from a preposterous story of Bishop Berkeley's producing a giant, to comments on the Druid religion; from descriptions of the revolutionary 'white boys', to a differentiation between various Irish beliefs in witches and fairies; from neo-classical ideas of landscape gardening, to anecdotes of Goldsmith picked up at Athlone from the widow of his former tutor in Trinity College.

After returning to Dublin early in November, Campbell devoted the last fifteen letters to a full discussion of the commercial, literary, artistic, and musical life in Ireland of the day. By this time he had given up the pose of being an objective English observer, and let himself go in an attempt to show the merits of his own country. He argued urgently for a commercial union of England and Ireland—always a topic near his heart—and gave many pages to the array of great men produced by Ireland in the past.

Campbell's special pleading and antiquarian specu-lations are of little interest to-day, but his general obser-vations are often amusing. Indeed, with a certain amount of judicious pruning the letters might still provide some entertainment, for Campbell's prose style at its best recalls the colloquial charm of Steele or Goldsmith. But this is to anticipate. Though first drafts of the letters were undoubtedly completed by December 1775, the entire work was not ready to show a publisher until the next October, when Campbell set out on his second trip to London.

Of this second visit, which was prolonged until May 1777, we know very little. No diary was kept, or, at least, none has survived. Boswell was absent from London the entire time, and Mrs Thrale does not mention Campbell in *Thraliana*.[1] Nevertheless, we know certainly that he sought out Dr Johnson on a number of occasions, for in a later publication Campbell refers to this winter in London when 'I had been honoured (and it is my pride to acknowledge it) with his familiarity and friendship'.[2] And late in the spring Johnson, in one of his own letters, specifically mentions a conversation with Campbell.[3]

Since the manuscript was accepted for publication by W. Strahan and T. Cadell, it is possible that Johnson may

[1] Mrs Thrale, during the late autumn and early winter of 1776–7, remained at Streatham, ill and dispirited, expecting the birth of another child.

[2] *Illustrations*, VII, 762. Taken from *Strictures*, p. 334.

[3] To Charles O'Connor, 19 May 1777 (*Life*, III, 111). See p. 13.

have lent a friendly hand in the negotiations. Certainly, Strahan helped Campbell to procure from Johnson a copy of his Latin epitaph on Goldsmith, which was inserted near the end of the volume, together with the footnote: 'Dr. Johnson has honoured the Publisher with a copy, though the epitaph is not yet finished, the identical spot where Goldsmith was born being not yet ascertained.'[1]

Actual printing of the volume was a slow process. Although the title-page carries the date 1777, the work did not appear until March 1778.[2] A Dublin reprint, which we may assume was issued shortly afterwards, is dated 1778.

The full title finally decided upon was *A Philosophical Survey of the South of Ireland, in a Series of Letters to John Watkinson, M.D.*, and in order to keep up the illusion of English authorship, the book (a substantial work of 476 pages, with plates) appeared anonymously—a device which later irritated Boswell, though he found the book itself 'very entertaining'.[3]

Campbell did not have to wait long for reviews. The *London Chronicle* for 28–31 March devoted its first page to a long quotation;[4] and in the *Critical Review* for April there was a five-page discussion. In general the reception was distinctly favourable. To be sure, the writer in the *Critical Review* was not deceived by the fiction of English

[1] P. 437. In the January, 1779, *Gent. Mag.* (xlix, 30), the Goldsmith epitaph is copied from the *Philosophical Survey*, the authorship of which is attributed to Watkinson. In the February issue (p. 85) the mistake is rectified and the epitaph translated.

[2] The *London Chronicle*, 17–19 Feb. 1778, lists the forthcoming volume; the 17–19 March issue advertises it as 'This day was published'.   [3] *Life*, ii, 339.

[4] The quotation is from Letter x, Kilkenny, 30 Aug. 1775.

authorship; moreover, as befitted the Scotch traditions of the periodical, the writer took Campbell to task for his scepticism concerning the poems of Ossian.[1] Except for making these qualifications, the reviewer was complimentary, describing the letters in the volume as 'written in an agreeable manner'. Much more tardy, the review by William Bewley in the *Monthly Review* did not appear until January 1779.[2]

The immediate reactions of his own countrymen, on the other hand, were not all favourable. Since some of his historical speculations were demonstrably wrong, and some of the comments on the social life of the inhabitants irritating to the people themselves, he was quickly plunged into a welter of controversy, from which he never quite emerged for the rest of his life. The first and cleverest attack came in an anonymous letter signed 'Nostradamus Hibernicus', which appeared in the *Hibernian Journal* for 13 May 1778. Written, as Campbell later found out, by one of the Fellows of Trinity, it was in imitation of Voltaire's ridicule of Rousseau. Many years later Campbell could admit that it was a 'really witty paper', but he also remembered that at the time the pointed ridicule made him 'wince'.[3]

As has been pointed out, the *Philosophical Survey* covered a variety of topics. Campbell's later interests tended more and more toward inquiries into the past. In May 1777 one of his last visits, before he returned to Ireland, was to Johnson, with whom he talked about

[1] *Critical Review*, XLV (April 1778), 252–6.
[2] *Monthly Review*, LX (Jan. 1779), 8–14. For the authorship of the review, see B.C. Nangle's *Index to the Monthly Review*.
[3] *Illustrations*, VII, 782–4.

the Irish antiquary, Charles O'Connor. Inspired by the conversation, Johnson wrote a letter to O'Connor on 19 May, intended to be carried by Campbell:

> ... I expected great discoveries in Irish antiquity, and large publications in the Irish language; but the world still remains as it was, doubtful and ignorant.... If you could give a history, though imperfect, of the Irish nation, from its conversion to Christianity to the invasion from England, you would amplify knowledge with new views and new objects. Set about it, therefore, if you can: do what you can easily do without anxious exactness. Lay the foundation, and leave the superstructure to posterity.[1]

No doubt Johnson gave similar advice to his visitor, for within the next decade Campbell decided to give the public a short history of the various revolutions in his native country. But he did not take the task very seriously, nor did he work at it to the exclusion of other interests.

During 1778 and the following years there are few references to Campbell in the surviving records. He was busy in local affairs—a few years before he had been made a Justice of the Peace for county Monaghan—and active in church matters: in 1779 he presented to his parish a beautiful communion chalice.[2] He wrote a short pamphlet on current affairs entitled *The First Lines of Ireland's Interest*, which was printed in Dublin;[3] and in 1780 printed a sermon: 'Preached in the Church of St Andrew's, Dublin, on Sunday the 6th of February, 1780, in aid of a

---

[1] *Life*, III, 111–12. See also II, 121.
[2] Leslie, *Clogher Clergy*, pp. 153, 264. He was made Justice of the Peace, 13 March 1776.
[3] On a copy in the Cambridge Univ. Library there is a manuscript note that the author was the 'Rev. Dr. Campbell'.

charitable Fund for the Support of twelve Boys and eight Girls.'[1]

It was not until June 1781, that Campbell again visited London, and this time only for a few weeks—just long enough to find a position for his nephew, John Thomas Campbell.[2] But even on such a hurried trip Campbell found time to call on Dr Johnson. On 11 June he went 'to pay him a morning visit'. 'I found him alone,' he later recorded, 'and nothing but mutual inquiries respecting mutual friends had passed, when Baretti came in.' Curious about conditions in Ireland, Baretti asked if the disturbances were over, at which Campbell launched into a defence of his countrymen. This stirred Johnson into a violent explosion. Campbell was so startled by Johnson's harsh attitude toward political revolutionaries that he could not forbear repeating the whole conversation to his good friend Dr Watkinson an hour or two later. Watkinson thought it 'so extraordinary', that he gave Campbell pen, ink, and paper 'to set it down immediately; for, says he, it deserves to be recorded, as a test of his political principles'. Years later, in explaining why he readily complied with the suggestion, Campbell attempted to soften the anecdote by adding that it 'discovers the original rectitude of a warm heart, biassed by national prejudices'.[3]

[1] It was listed in the *Monthly Review* for May 1780 (LXII, 414) where the sermon was called 'ingenious and sensible'.

[2] Son of William Campbell, Thomas Campbell's younger brother. This was the nephew who later took the Diary to New South Wales. For information about William and his family see H. B. Swanzy, *The Vicars of Newry*, pp. 15–20. See also D. A. Chart, *The Drennan Letters*, p. 22. See *Diary*, p. 94.

[3] *Strictures on the History of Ireland*, p. 336; reprinted in *Illustrations*, VII, 762–4. For Campbell's account of the conversation, see pp. 94–6.

Dr Thomas Campbell

Campbell had always been interested in the economic needs of his country. In the *Philosophical Survey* he had argued cogently for a trade union with England; later, in 1782, he became embroiled in a pamphlet war over problems of unfair excise taxes on Irish distilleries. His first blast, *A Letter to His Grace the Duke of Portland, Lord Lieutenant of Ireland*, so irked the government authorities that it was answered immediately by a writer for the Board of Revenue. Campbell's opponent set forth the official point of view and caustically referred to the misrepresentation ' by Newspaper writers and Gentlemen who write Pamphlets on subjects of which they are ignorant, or which if they understand they intentionally misrepresent'.[1] Campbell promptly replied with another pamphlet bearing the resounding title, *A Remedy for the Distilleries of Ireland, Which, at Present, Labour under Such Disadvantages, As to Be Called a Disease, in an Official Pamphlet, Just Published, Intitled Observations on a Letter to the Duke of Portland, Lord Lieutenant of Ireland, So Far As the Same Relates to the Subject of Revenue, &c.*, by the Author of the Letter to the Duke of Portland, Dublin, 1783.[2]

Such anonymous diversions may have added to Campbell's repute in the small circle of Dublin literati,

[1] A copy is preserved in the Cambridge Univ. Library. The full title is *Observations on a Pamphlet Entitled a Letter to His Grace the Duke of Portland, Lord Lieutenant of Ireland, So Far As the Same Relates to the Subject of Revenue; in Which Is Considered the State of the Distilling Trade of Ireland*, Dublin, 1782. The ascription of the earlier pamphlet to Campbell is made because of a manuscript note on his reply. See n. 2.
[2] On a copy in the Cambridge Univ. Library is written in a contemporary hand: 'By the Revd Tho. Campbell L.L.D. Chancellor of Glogher &c He died about the middle of July, 1795.'

15

but his general reputation rested upon his skill as a preacher.[1] In later years the numerous requests he received to preach special 'Charity sermons' show that he was recognised as one of the best pulpit orators in the country.

In 1783 Campbell received an offer to co-operate in a new edition of William Camden's *Britannia*, a chorographical description of England, Scotland, and Ireland from the earliest antiquity. In addition to printing Camden's original Latin text, the new editor, Richard Gough, planned to include all the information he could secure about each individual county. When he approached Lord Dacre for material about Ireland, he was referred at once to Campbell as 'more knowing in the antiquities and particularities of that kingdom than most of its best-informed natives'.[2] Moreover, Lord Dacre actively urged Campbell to aid in the undertaking.

Little urging was needed. Knowing well the deficiencies of the older work, Campbell commented to Lord Dacre that Ireland 'was treated with little exactness by *Cambden* which occasioned an old *Distich* the point of which was "that when *Cambden* wrote of *England* he had two *eyes* when of *Scotland* one only but that he had none at all when he wrote of Ireland".'[3] He added: 'As soon as I can collect my thoughts I shall endeavour to throw together those hints your friend wishes relative to the several articles specified.'

As he found opportunity during the next months, Campbell set to work on the scattered notes which he

[1] See D. A. Chart's *The Drennan Letters*, p. 22.
[2] *Illustrations*, vii, 797.
[3] The original letter, dated 17 May 1783, and the earliest known letter of Campbell to survive, is now in the Bodleian.

thought Gough might wish to use. But he was not too sure they were all suitable. 'My mode of writing may not perhaps please Mr. Gough,' he wrote to Lord Dacre,

for I cannot help making some reflections as I go along, for which perhaps he would not choose to be responsible. However, if any thing of that kind occurs, I would rather he should use my name than suppress those ideas, which I, as an Irishman, might think necessary to be inserted.[1]

For the next two years Campbell supplied Gough with all the data he could find, but he also had other plans of his own. Remembering Dr Johnson's suggestion of a popular survey of Irish history, he had collected almost enough material by the autumn of 1786 for a single volume. Accordingly, early in October he set out for Scotland, and thence to London, where he soon found that the English booksellers were not very encouraging about his proposed 'History of the Revolutions of Ireland'. There had been so many 'paltry productions' on the subject that the general public was prejudiced against any work on Irish history, and furthermore the publishers feared that all profit might be lost because of pirated Dublin editions.

Temporarily discouraged, Campbell was glad to drive up to Scotland with his friend Sir Capel Molyneux, planning later to return to London to make an explicit arrangement with some bookseller. But when a talk with an Icelandic authority convinced him that more evidence might be found concerning the early part of his history, Campbell decided to accompany Molyneux all the way to Ireland. Since all his papers had been left in London, for the time being little could be done on the history. Instead, he spent the winter, as usual, in Dublin dabbling in various

[1] *Illustrations*, vii, 798. Letter of 7 Jan. 1784.

antiquarian researches, and the spring and early summer superintending the building of a gallery in his church at Killeevan.

From 1787 we have fuller evidence of Campbell's activities, largely through a series of letters written to Bishop Percy.[1] To Percy he wrote about common antiquarian interests, church problems, and of his own literary projects. To Percy also he commented on the ominous political rumblings in Ireland, and on the other topics of the day. They are pleasant, well expressed letters, which give an admirable picture of the writer—friendly, obliging, volatile, a trifle given to procrastination, and perhaps unduly obsequious.

The letters also contain additional information about Campbell's trip to France in the summer of 1787 (see pp. 99–102). Setting out for London early in June, he stayed there only a short time—long enough to dine several times with John Pinkerton, the Scotch antiquary, and to confer with Gough about the *Britannia*. Since his own proposed volume had not been eagerly taken by a publisher, Campbell generously offered to assist the editor in drawing up an account of the government of Ireland since the time of Camden to the present. Then late in the month he crossed over to Calais, and through Boulogne to Paris.

Not being able either to speak or to understand the language, Campbell at first was so disgusted with France that, together with some other British travellers, he decided to leave forthwith. But soon he became acquainted with some Parisians who spoke English—one a

[1] Printed by Nichols in *Illustrations*, vii, 759–96. Four letters were first printed in *Gent. Mag.* cii (Nov. 1832), 409–11.

Dr Thomas Campbell

fascinating lady who knew Mrs Montagu and the English Bluestockings—and his whole attitude changed. In fact, he enjoyed himself so much that he finally left Paris 'with regret, bewailing my sad fate that I did not understand (or rather speak) the language of a people who know the value of words so well, and whose peculiar felicity it seems to be *savoir vivre*'. And he had learned 'never more to pass a censure from a transient view of persons or things'.

Campbell's entries in his *Diary* during this visit—by no means as full or as entertaining as those made twelve years before in London—show the same mixture of praise and blame. Indeed, one attribute which made Campbell a good diarist was his willingness to set down conflicting prejudices and enthusiasms just as they came to him, and without reticence or thoughts of decorum. What he disliked he attacked; what he liked he warmly recommended. Consequently, we may lament the meagre quantity of his entries, and wish he had given us more anecdotes such as that included in a later letter to Percy about the elderly Parisian salonière whom Campbell visited. One day in explaining his failure to pay regular morning visits, as she had recommended, he told her that two or three priests had obligingly conducted him about Paris. She exclaimed:

Good God, Signior Anglois, keep company with priests!— why, if you keep company with priests, nobody will keep company with you. Priests! the poorest creatures in the world, creatures who know nothing but a point here or a point there, and no matter whether the point be here or there, for it is worth nothing in itself; but then Irish priests! the foolishest of all priests, *the very Swisses of theology*.[1]

[1] *Illustrations*, VII, 770.

Dr Thomas Campbell

Campbell remained for about a month in Paris. Then, on 1 August he crossed to Brighton, where he surveyed the British nobility with a somewhat jaundiced eye, and thence through London back to Clones. On the way he stopped at Beaconsfield to visit Edmund Burke, who was so much interested in the proposed History of the Revolutions of Ireland that he presented his visitor not only with good advice but also with his own valuable collection of Irish manuscripts. Campbell left with four large folio volumes and a head full of new plans.[1]

Since Campbell's general idea had been to 'give the spirit rather than the letter' of the melancholy annals of his country, Burke's advice to be as brief as possible upon everything before Henry II was readily accepted. Availing himself of the new evidence, and weeding out certain material which he had formerly planned to use, he spent the next few months working at his survey.

It must be remembered that Campbell's ideas about his fellow-historians had changed materially in the preceding decade. In the *Philosophical Survey* he had been eulogistic about the well-known authority, Vallancey, and in his early conversation with Johnson had been unstinted in his praise of O'Connor. But subsequent researches had tended to make him suspicious of what he thought to be their fanciful reconstructions of the distant past. Bishop Percy described what was going on to Pinkerton:

Dr. Campbell is supposed to be now engaged in researches, which, like a talisman, will tend to dissolve the unsubstantial visions and reveries of Colonel Vallancey and his followers. He is a very careful and cautious inquirer into the reliques of antiquity.[2]

[1] *Illustrations*, vii, 773.　　　[2] *Ibid.* viii, 135 (28 Feb. 1787).

Dr Thomas Campbell

From the mass of letters between Gough and his correspondents—Joseph Cooper Walker, John Pinkerton, and the Rev. Edward Ledwich—from Campbell's letters to Percy and Gough, all conveniently published later by Nichols,[1] we can piece together Campbell's multifarious activities for the next few years. During the autumn of 1787 he seems to have been working in a desultory way on the projected accounts for Gough, and also, in order to 'expose the inconsistencies' of the accepted authorities, he wrote a short sketch of the Ecclesiastical and Literary History of Ireland down to the establishment of the National Church. This sketch, under the signature of 'Jerneus', appeared in the *Dublin Chronicle* for 24 and 27 December.[2] Later, as he told Percy, he expected to revise it for a separate publication.

Meanwhile, to his surprise and chagrin, he had heard nothing further from Gough. But when he arrived in Dublin in February for his annual winter visit, he found to his astonishment an angry letter from Gough about some proof-sheets sent over for correction in the preceding summer. Campbell answered at once, explaining that until then he had received nothing from Gough, and begging for more time in which to correct the numerous errors in the enclosed sheets, particularly in the pages referring to the Constitution of Ireland which were 'such a jumble of times and circumstances as would disgrace so fine a work'. Gough, he found, had quoted extensively from portions of the *Philosophical Survey*. But Campbell's ideas on many matters had changed in the intervening

[1] In vols. VII and VIII of the *Illustrations*. In the following pages individual references will not be given for each quotation.
[2] Mentioned in *Illustrations*, VII, 775.

21

years, and he confessed he would be sorry 'to be responsible for many opinions' to be found in it. Instead, he pleaded for a few weeks more, promising 'upon the honour of a man and the credit of a writer' to send Gough 'a sketch of the Irish Constitution, at sight of which both you and I would be sorry for having resorted to the "Philosophical Survey"'.

In a curt reply Gough granted another month's respite. On 20 February Campbell wrote again:

Notwithstanding an illness since I wrote last to you, and though I had not a book on the subject in Dublin, I inclose you by this post part of a sketch (not half finished), to show you I have not been quite idle....I assure you that I have refused to preach no less than two charity sermons before May next, merely that I have more leisure to serve your work....

Two weeks later he added that the remainder of the 'Sketch' would be sent shortly. It was, Campbell confessed, 'the skeleton of that history which I mean to publish'.

At the same time, in order to allay the distant editor's fears, Joseph Cooper Walker also wrote to Gough:

Dr. Campbell has been indefatigable in your service. He has drawn up for your use an admirable Memoir on the Constitution of Ireland, in fact, the only regular account of the constitution that has ever been prepared. It will be a bright ornament to your work. He expects it will be printed exactly as it is written. Indeed, it will not admit of being more compressed.

By April, nevertheless, relations were again so strained that in one note Campbell wrote to Gough in the third person. The correspondence continued through the spring with increasing irritability on both sides and in July Gough was still begging for the completion of one of

Dr Thomas Campbell

Campbell's contributions. It was not until June 1789, that the three folio volumes of the *Britannia* appeared. Fortunately, by this time Gough's irritation had completely vanished and his references to Campbell in the Preface and the Acknowledgements are cordial and complimentary.[1]

Even before the *Britannia* was published, Campbell was at work on a volume of his own which was to be a *pot pourri* of all that he had lately been writing. As he explained to Percy, 'I have a notion of republishing "Jerneus" in a volume, next spring, after revising and correcting it'; and to this he intended to add a corrected version of his contributions to Gough's work. Being intended to embody in a single volume all Campbell's doubts about Vallancey and his supporters, the work was deliberately controversial in tone. It was merely to serve as a preliminary to his *magnum opus*.

It is not clear exactly when the book was published, but the Dublin edition is dated 1789, and was probably issued sometime in the autumn of that year.[2] The long eighteenth-century title gives a summary of the contents: *Strictures on the Ecclesiastical and Literary History of Ireland: from the Most Ancient Times till the Introduction of the Roman Ritual, and the Establishment of Papal Supremacy, by Henry II King of England. Also, an*

[1] The *St James's Chronicle* for 6–9 June 1789 lists the *Britannia* as 'This day was published'. Campbell's 'Historical Sketch' appeared in vol. III, pp. 481–8*. In the Preface (I, v) Gough speaks of Campbell's 'excellent performance', etc. Campbell is favourably mentioned in the review of *Britannia* in the *Monthly Review*, new series, III (Oct. 1790), 175–87.
[2] 8vo, 418 pages. Printed for Luke White, No. 86 Dame Street, Dublin, and dedicated to Edmund Burke.

Dr Thomas Campbell

Historical Sketch of the Constitution and Government of Ireland, from the Most Early Authenticated Period down to the Year 1783. This time Campbell's name appears boldly on the title-page.

Once the Dublin printing was ready, Campbell set out for London late in December to arrange for an English edition. Together with some Dublin friends he spent Christmas in Bath, and then shortly afterwards went on to London. Of the remainder of his stay there in January 1790 we know nothing, except that he was able to get the well-known publishers, G. G. J. and J. Robinson, in Paternoster Row to issue his *Strictures*. He was certainly back in Ireland long before the first comments on his work began to appear in print.

As before, the London reviews were gratifying—the references lengthy and highly complimentary. Perhaps the fact that the book was critical of Irish chauvinism recommended it to English readers; or perhaps it was Campbell's highly sceptical attitude which was relished, so long as it was applied to non-English topics. At any rate, the writers for the *Monthly Review*, the *Critical Review*, and the *Gentleman's Magazine* were united in praise of the author and his historical approach.[1] In the *Gentleman's Magazine* Gough described the work of his former helper with friendly partisanship: 'One stroke of Dr. C's discerning pen does away all the visionary lumber that modern antiquaries have heaped up, round, and upon, the foundation' of the old authorities. Vallancey and O'Connor, Gough insisted, were 'driven from their

[1] *Monthly Review*, I, 2nd series (Feb. 1790), 150–6; *Gent. Mag.* LX (April 1790), 318–19, 333–7. Professor B.C. Nangle tells me that the reviewer in the *Monthly* was probably John Noorthouck.

Dr Thomas Campbell

strongholds of fanciful and far-fetched etymology, charlatanery in antiquities', and all their attempts to impose on the credulous in an enlightened age.[1]

In the English press, at least, Campbell won a victory over his opponents. Of course, Vallancey retorted with acrimony;[2] but intelligent men of his own day and succeeding generations have in general agreed that Campbell was on the right track. Had his *Strictures* been more systematic, more accurate, and less purely controversial, he might even have won a secure place as a critical historian. But the book had many weaknesses which are summed up in a letter from Ledwich to Percy, written many years later:

> Campbell was my particular friend for near 30 years. His 'Strictures' are a hasty performance. I pointed out some hundreds of necessary corrections; and one day, from twelve till we went to dinner, I spent in authenticating what I objected to; had he lived, I am sure he would have new-written the whole. The booksellers are about a new edition, and beg my assistance; this I would willingly give, but there are too many things rash and unfounded to correct, which would injure the reputation of the man I very much esteemed.[3]

Campbell's next literary venture was the direct result of his growing friendship with Bishop Percy. For fifteen years Percy had been planning a life of Goldsmith, to be prefixed to an edition of his works.[4] As far back as 1775,

---

[1] In the same issue of the *Gent. Mag.* (April 1790) a writer who signed himself 'K.T.' highly commended the volume, though calling part of it 'ingenious, but superficial'.

[2] In the Appendix to the fifth volume of his *Collectanea*.

[3] *Illustrations*, VII, 826. Letter of 24 Oct. 1802.

[4] K.C. Balderston, *The History and Sources of Percy's Memoir of Goldsmith*, Cambridge, 1926. See also T. Shearer and A. Tillotson, 'Percy's Relations with Cadell and Davies', *The Library*, XV

Dr Thomas Campbell

Campbell had heard about the plan, but in the intervening years Percy had done little except collect material. Perhaps because he now felt that popular literary pursuits were not consistent with his episcopal duties, Percy was determined not to have his name appear as author of the Memoir of Goldsmith. Instead, he decided to delegate the work to a sub-editor who would be subject to the Bishop's censorship, and would bear the brunt of any unfavourable criticism. Campbell's energy, his fluent style, and his sceptical common sense recommended him for the post.

Exactly when Campbell and Percy agreed on the plan is not known, but it may have been in Dublin in February 1790.[1] Just back from London where he had made the final arrangements for the English edition of his *Strictures*, Campbell was ready and eager for a new project. Willingly he took charge of the manuscripts and anecdotes which Percy had collected; and as soon as he returned to Clones in March began work on the writing. On 6 April he commented that he had 'sketched out a sort of exordium to the Life'; then he asked if he might mention Percy's name as the source of some of the anecdotes.

It will procure the work a more favourable reading, and will give me more credit. I trust it shall be conducted in such a manner as not to make you blush; but it will be always in your own power to expunge or add till it can be wrought into some shape that will no way disgust you.

(Sept. 1934), 224–36. It was once thought that fear of attacks by Ritson was responsible for Percy's retiring from the literary scene, but it now seems more probable (as Professor D. Nichol Smith tells me) that after Percy became a Bishop he thought it incumbent on him to give up all literary pursuits.

[1] Percy was in Dublin in February. See *Illustrations*, VIII, 276.

Dr Thomas Campbell

Throughout the spring Campbell was busy on the work, and on 16 June he wrote:

> Goldsmith's Life goes on without much interruption, though I am now deep in mortar, and employ masons by the day (in order that it may be executed in the best manner) in the building of my church, of which I take upon me to be architect and overseer. And at intervals I retire from this employment, sometimes vexatious enough, to write a paragraph as a recreation. N.B. The site of the church is but two or three hundred yards from my house.[1]
>
> I have *him* now in London, and am endeavouring to recollect your first visit to him, when the loan, or repayment, of the chamber-pot of coals was asked....

In this and succeeding letters to Percy, Campbell is full of questions and active in borrowing volumes—as well he might be, since he had never known Goldsmith personally, and since he confessed that he had never 'read a line of his dramatic works'. Again, on 30 June, Campbell pleaded for the right to use Percy's name in one of the anecdotes, but humbly explained, 'in this as every thing else, your wish shall be a command'. Later he added:

> Having mentioned Griffiths, I will confess to you that the circumstance of him and his wife (I mean their altering and interpolating Goldsmith's criticisms on books for the Review) puzzles me. It is one of the most valuable anecdotes before me, and my conscience bids me report it, but my fears whisper to me that all the Reviews will abuse me for so doing. But *who's afraid*? Yes, I am; but it is that I am tormenting you.

---

[1] See E. P. Shirley, *History of the County of Monaghan*, London, 1879, pp. 335–7. Campbell's church in townland Shanco was begun in 1790. It is now a ruin. On the tower is an inscription in Latin indicating the year of construction, and also containing Campbell's name as rector. The present church of Killeevan, whose east window commemorates Campbell, was built in 1857–8.

Dr Thomas Campbell

During the summer the work on his church occupied so much of his time that early in August Campbell had to admit that he had not written 'a line for Goldsmith this month and more'. Nevertheless, by 9 September he evidently believed that most of the work was done.

My greatest difficulty now is to have it transcribed so as that your Lordship could cast an eye over it. I have tried one or two country schoolmasters, but, though they can write, they cannot read—my writing.

It seems evident that only Mrs Percy's illness stood in the way of their taking the papers to London for alterations before publication. Since her health did not rapidly improve, Campbell instead took the manuscript to Dromore for consultation. Here Percy indicated all the corrections he wished, and the work was considered tentatively complete.

In the spring of 1791 Percy took his family to Bath, in the hope that the waters would improve Mrs Percy's health. Later in the summer he suggested that Campbell should join him in England in order that the arrangements for publication might be completed. But various things kept Campbell in Ireland. In the first place, as he explained on 13 August: 'The steeple of my church (to be executed with hewn stone) would probably be bungled in the execution (as was the case with that part of the church done in my late absence in Dublin).' Moreover, he was involved in family affairs concerning the guardianship of a nephew, which had resulted in a lawsuit in Dublin. So he was forced to wait at least until autumn. 'Then I shall take with me all the documents respecting Goldsmith, and shall, please God, be in London early in November.'

Dr Thomas Campbell

Again he was delayed. The lawsuit dragged on in Dublin through November; then, with bad weather and the holidays approaching, he thought it best to return home. It was not until 3 February 1792 that he could write from Dublin that he was on his way to London at last, and with the suggestion that during March he might go ahead with 'printing off the first sheets', while sending the proofs to Percy at Bath. At the same time he admitted:

I have not opened those papers since I left Dromore, leaving whatever alterations are to be further made for the immediate press copy, with which I could wish to furnish the printer, not altogether, but as he shall want it; so that while I am inserting such circumstances as seem rightly stated by Boswell [whose *Life of Johnson* had recently appeared], and writing it out fair, the printer may be going on with the beginning, in which you think no alterations, but such as you have noted, need be made.

Late in February Campbell reached Bath where he remained for three weeks visiting with the Percys. Here he met an old acquaintance not seen for many years—the former Mrs Thrale, now Mrs Piozzi. Together they laughed over stories of old times,[1] and Campbell used the opportunity to collect some further anecdotes about Goldsmith. Mrs Piozzi was so much interested that she wrote at once to Arthur Murphy in London for confirmation of some of the matters discussed. Murphy replied:

I have not a very good recollection of Doct.^r Campbell, but I suppose that at your house I was formerly acquainted with him. If you supply him with any materials for the Life of Goldsmith, what you mention about his Envy at seeing the

---

[1] *Thraliana*, ii, 835; John Rylands Library, English MS. 548–6; letter to Hester Maria Thrale, 23 April 1796 (see n. 1, p. 1).

hat, and also the Preface, in which He was *wildly appealing to Posterity*, is perfectly true; But that Preface, as you well distinguish, had nothing to [do] with his Essays.[1]

Murphy then gave an amusing account of the opening night of *The Good Natured Man* and Goldsmith's erratic behaviour on that occasion. 'This is the story, which, if you please, you may dress up for Doct.ʳ Campbell, in your own manner, which is allways Extremely happy.'

Campbell had come to England this time fully expecting to begin the actual printing of the Memoir, but instead trouble developed with John Nichols, who was to be the publisher, and the project was delayed indefinitely.[2] As a result, Campbell went up to London from Bath on 19 March, stayed there less than a week, and was back in Ireland by the 31st.

The rest of the story is soon told. Just before Percy returned to Ireland in the summer of 1793, after two years in England, he transferred the project from Nichols to Murray. Then in November Murray suddenly died. Before Percy was able to give further time in England to the affair, Campbell himself was dead. It was not until seven years after his death that the Memoir finally appeared.

The last few years of Campbell's life were far from happy. The world was out of joint, and Ireland itself was stirring with vague rumblings which menaced his very existence. His old care-free pleasant life was coming to an end. To be sure, he continued to work at what was to

[1] John Rylands Library, English MS. 548–6.
[2] Percy was determined to have Goldsmith's relatives get some cash payment from the edition, while the trade was only willing to give unbound copies to be sold in Ireland for their benefit. See n. 4, p. 25.

be his *magnum opus*—the History of the Revolutions of Ireland—but with little zest. Though two early parts had actually been roughly printed in Dublin some years before, the entire work was never completed.[1] With another terrifying revolution just about to break, he could scarcely concentrate on writing of those in the distant past.

Like his friend Burke, Campbell was shocked by what was going on in France, and by what he called 'that cursed democratic rage' which was spreading throughout his own country. Everywhere he saw ruin confronting his own class. We can see his state of mind in his one published work of the early nineties—a charity sermon preached in the church at Gallown. In September 1793 he wrote to Percy:

My Sermon will be a very long one, and, I suppose, very tedious, if not displeasing to some, for, contrary to my original intention, it has taken a political direction, in opposition to that foolish and wicked doctrine of the equality of men and their rights.

The discourse was given on 6 October, and printed in Dublin early the next year. A strange hotch-potch of religious commentary, statistical arguments concerning charitable projects, and political fulminations, it is perhaps best summed up in the author's own postscript:

If it should be asked, is this heterogeneous discourse a sermon, or a pamphlet? Is it one, or is it many? It will be answered, that unity of subject was not originally aimed at. Yet to inculcate the utility of new churches and charitable loans, was, at first, all that was intended. The composition, however, affected by the times, took a political turn. And, on

---

[1] *Illustrations*, VII, 772, 776.

reviewing the principles, there laid down, they appear, to a partial eye, as containing a refutation (perhaps too abstracted) of the delirious doctrines of the natural equality and equal rights of man. Under this impression the discourse is now printed, with all its imperfections on its head.[1]

Physically Campbell had never been a brave man. The 'pet sheep' of Boswell's description was not temperamentally suited to the rough dangers of a revolutionary uprising. The scholarly battles of antiquaries were more to his taste. Yet there was no ivory tower in Northern Ireland into which to retire. With trouble brewing all about him, his letters to Percy became more and more agitated. By early 1795 conditions were fast approaching a climax, the rebellion at first taking the form of a total withholding of the payment of tithes to the established church. The mob threatened to burn down the house of any juror who dared adjudge the tithe as due; the proctors sent out with processes were unmercifully stripped and beaten, and then threatened with death if they came again. In his own parish at Clones, the proctors, forced to tear up the processes themselves, refused to proceed with any presentation. Seeing the contagion spreading on all sides, Campbell spent his time calling for troops and planning the building of a local barracks to house them.

To be sure, he did not apprehend any immediate general slaughter as in France. As he wrote to Percy in April:

[1] The complete title of the sermon as printed was *A Discourse Delivered in the New Church of St. Luke's, Gallown, on Sunday the 6th of October* 1793; *When a Collection Was Made, in order to Extend the Benefits of a Charitable Loan of Fifty Guineas, Already Lent out to Industrious Housekeepers of the Parish of Gallown.* Printed by Bonham; Mercier & Co., Booksellers, Dublin, 1794.

Dr Thomas Campbell

You know that my fears have long bordered on timidity; but, though I feared robbery, murder, associations against tithe, &c. I never suspected a general insurrection could take place on any contingency but that of a French invasion....In that case, indeed, I am persuaded that the country is so organized by their committees that there might be a general rising....

To make matters worse, Campbell's health was now rapidly failing. In Dublin during the winter he had been very ill, and in the spring was little better. Worry over his future income, over the prospects for his country, combined to keep him 'always croaking'. Pathetically, he was almost glad that he would probably not long have to struggle with a world gone mad. 'I begin to console myself', he wrote to Percy, 'under that malady which so much alarmed me when in Dublin—as I would not wish long to survive my means of existence.' Worn out, disillusioned and discouraged, he did not much care what happened to him, so long as it came soon. And he did not have long to wait. Late in the spring, probably to consult other medical opinion, he set out for London. There on 20 June 1795 he died at the age of sixty-two.[1]

Campbell's death stirred scarcely a ripple in the full tide of British life. Indeed, his passing is not even mentioned in the *Gentleman's Magazine*. His scholarly friends sincerely mourned the kindly, impulsive man; and his congregation in the little country church at Killeevan no doubt missed his bustling activity. But what of literary fame? What of all the glorious plans for the *magnum opus*? What of his immediate reputation as an Irish historian?

[1] *Illustrations*, VII, 795–6; *Correspondence of John Pinkerton*, 1830, I, 390; Leslie, *Clogher Clergy*, p. 62.

Dr Thomas Campbell

Here fortune was against him. To be sure, his friend Ledwich considered trying to bring out the projected 'Revolutions of Ireland', but the work was too fragmentary to produce a creditable volume.[1] And, as we have already seen, despite his high esteem of the man, Ledwich considered it advisable even to discourage a proposed reprinting of the *Strictures*. Campbell had obviously failed in his literary quest. To his contemporaries he was an amiable, ingenious scholar, a useful clergyman and philanthropist, and a valuable critic of historical research; they would not, however, have regarded him as having done anything worthy of lasting remembrance. But they reckoned without a little battered note-book, filled with scrawled records of the conversation of a great man, which would one day gain another hearing for the forgotten antiquary.

[1] On 7 August 1795 J. C. Walker wrote to Pinkerton about Campbell: 'You will lament with me the death of the author. His Revolutions of Ireland (part of which is already printed) will, I believe, be edited by Mr Ledwich, a writer with whose merits you are not unacquainted.' (*Pinkerton Correspondence*, I, 390.) On the other hand, it is not clear that any of Campbell's work was ever issued.

THOMAS CAMPBELL'S
DIARY

A NOTE ON THE TEXT

P u n c t u a t i o n and spelling have been transcribed exactly as they appear in the original manuscript. One exception is that the old contraction 'thorn-e', which Campbell used almost exclusively in place of 'the', has been recorded as 'the'. The form 'ye', sometimes employed by modern printers, does not accurately represent the proper pronunciation, and is misleading. Other contractions, however, have not been normalised. Where a spelling is uncertain or not easily deciphered, a question mark, inside brackets, is placed after the best possible reconstruction.

In an attempt to make the account strictly chronological, various separate sheets which were found in a pocket of the original Diary have been inserted where they appear to belong. In each instance a note explains the insertion.

THE *DIARY*

F E B R Y 23 D 1775   I went aboard the Besborough pacquet & weighed anchor at five in the evening—& landed at Hollyhead at eight oclock next morning— which was very foggy & hazy. The passage was on a very pacific sea. So that I was so little affected with sickness as to lament the want of that substitute for hippo (1)—Here we breafasted & the eggs were so small that I had curiosity to measure them & the longest diameter was 1¾ of an inch—Here is a odd old Church in the form of a cross—In the yard of which Flood &

Dr Campbell's Diary

Agar fought about seven years ago—but the feud did not
end there—agar at length fell by this his antagonist
A.D. 1769 (2)—The folks at the Inn told me that the
weather had been generally hazy for a month past & they
expected it w^d be so till March—They had but two or
three days of frost last winter—The Saylors say it is
always foggy when the wind is at south—The Church is
on the outside of an H-like figure i.e. the old part which
is not ugly & seems the remains of something greater—
there is an addition however of modern work.

From Holyhead to Bangor is a country not unlike that
about Virginia in the county Cavan—As you approach
Bangors ferry the prospect brightens & becomes agree-
ably varyed with hill & dale & sea—But the first view
of Bangor itself is so transcendantly beautiful that it
beggars the richness of words. I never was so wrapped
with surprize as when this lovely vista struck my ravished
sight. And every step I took so altered the contour that
it became a new scene of wonder, & the last was still
more pleasing than the first; for the distant view of Beau-
morris & the circumjacent hills afforded so fine & airy
a back ground that I never saw one so picturesque. I have
heard Englishmen say that Ireland had finer subjects for
the Landcape painter that England. But sure they have
not taken in Wales. Bangor alone w^d yield an infinitude
of scenes. Let those Painters who affect composition
study & imitate Bangor—They may avail themselves of
it as Michael Angelo did of the Dorso—At Pinman-
muir (3) Nature hath painted with her boldest pencil; nor
hath she neglected the graces in the lower grounds;
there are great elegancies in the vally which dulcify the

Facsimile of the first page of the Diary

(The so-called facsimile included in the edition of 1854 is a crude and inaccurate drawing)

stupendous cragginess of the mountain—The Cathedral
of Bangor looks somewhat to a mere Irish eye—The
Choir has been glazed with painted glass & if the Church
was ceiled it w^d add much to the beauty of it. But it must
not be forgotten that here in the short time I spent in it—
(which was during a stop the Postillion made to get a
pair of boots) I had an opportunity of observing a sad
remnant of Popish superstion performed in this Cathedral. I observed a vast crowd both in the quire & body
of the Church, & the surpliced minister standing at the
Chancel. I mixed in the crowd, & each person according
(I suppose) to his ability went up to the chancel table &
there made his offering. I saw however nothing but
half-pence & at first wondered what all this could mean,
but returning I saw a corpse lying in the Isle of the
church. And this brought to my mind the account which
Hughes the Welshman gave of the great benefits arising
from funerals &c This was evidently a relick of the
offerings for praying the soul out of Purgatory—NB. The
distance from Holyhead to Bangor ferry is 25 miles—
from thence to Conway 18—a postshay & four from
Holyhead is 8 guineas for 2 & 9 for 3—from Conway to
St. asaph is 18 miles—At Bangor ferry we c^d get no beer,
yet one w^d think the tempering of Mault & hops into
that consistence were a facile operation—nor was there
meat except eggs & rashers of beef—At Conway both
meat & drink were as bad as we could meet in any Irish Inn

FEBRY 25 VIZ. SATURDAY The foggy gloom was
dispelled about 7 in the morning by a sight of the Sun
who gilded the horors of the mountains—Even deserted
Conway smoothed its frowning brow. The Castle &

wood have a good effect from the water—but the tri-
angular fortification with its flankers inclosing such a
poor pittance of wooden houses looks miserable—The
beauty of the prospect vanishes in the ratio of the distance—After shuddering in walking over the cliffe at
Panmanross we were regaled with passing thro' the vally
of Cluen & thence to St Asaph—where we breakfasted,
& here for the first time did we find any thing like that
English neatness I had heard so much of—The house
was Thompsons some distance from the town—which
hindered me from looking into the Cathedral & the
Parish Church—The Cathedral was a cross with the
steeple in the middle not unlike the cathedral of Armagh—
The Bridge was composed of the flat elliptic arches, &
seemed en passant to be very elegant—The Town itself
seems poor & little

On the 25th we got into Chester at 8 oclock at night—
Chester is built of wood chiefly & is surrounded with a
wall which affords an agreeable walk flagged about four
feet broad, the periphery of which is 1¾ & 101 yds—The
Dee winds prettily round one side of the town, & a canal
through a rock is now a cutting round the other. NB
there are nine churches in Chester, yet the town is small
in comparison of Bermingham. The Cathedral of St Wer-
burghs is worth seeing, especially the quire, which is
ornamented with oak beautifully carved—The old Cloysters still remain & have a venerable appearance—There
has been an old Abbey—The Bishop's house fronts the
Abby square

From Chester to Bermingham (75 miles) we arrived
at near one oclock at night on the 26—Whitchurch

(20 miles from Chester) is a pretty clean old town, & Newport (41 from D?) neither so large nor so clean—here we met several people very drunk—this we supposed was owing to the festivity on the sunday—and now the night wrapped the sweet country of Stafford & Warwickshire from my longing eyes—NB. Chetwind a country seat about 2 miles from Newport was very neat

FEBY 27TH we stayed at Bermingham till after 12, & drove to Henly viz. 14 miles in less than 1½—Bermingham is large populous & clean—St Phillip's church & steeple is a beautiful building of Hewn stone & very modern—The steeple of the octagonal Church is exquisitely beautiful & the spire of Martins not ugly—The number of Churches I c^d not learn from our boot catch guide, but there were four at least beside many other places of worship—The town however cannot contain 150000 nor above ⅓ of that number, yet they contend that next to London it is the most populous town &c—That part of Warwickshire from Bermingham to Stradford upon Avon seems to be a poor wet clay, for on the commons it is a mixture of rushes & heath, but on the adjacent parts they are obliged to lay down the ground in prodigious broad ridges to deepen & dry the soil. At Stratford I was amply rewarded by diverting from the great London road, for there I saw the tomb of Shakespeare, was in the room wherein he was born & sat in his chair &c &c   Stratford is an antient town built mostly of wood, & seems now in a deserted state, without any manufacture but the woolcoming—of which trade Shakepear originally was—There is a handsome Town house

Dr Campbell's Diary

lately built at the expense of the corporation & neighbouring gentlemen—in a nitch whereof a statue of Shakespear, the gift of Mr Garrick stands. In the great room of it are two pictures one of Shakespear by Wilson the gift also of Garrick; & another of Garrick himself embracing the bust of Shakespear by Gainsborough done at the charge of the corporation. The house where Shakespear died stood near the beautiful old chapel in the middle of the town, & in the garden belonging grew the famous Mulberry tree, whereof I saw a box in a toy shop there. (4) The Church is large consisting of a large Ayle & a Choire—In both of which there are several monumental inscriptions—Shakespears tombstone lies at the chancel of the choir, with his own two lines denouncing curses on him who shall move his bones (5)— by the way I conceive the reason of this curse &c was a custom which has been observed at Stratford of collecting the bones of the dead & throwing them into a vault under the steeple—The monument raised by his wife consisting of a half length figure &c &c is intirely Gothic, but not more so than the inscription under it (6)—On the right of chancel lyeth a monumental statue in an horizontal posture with precatory hands &c of John Combe— on which Shakespear wrote his famous distich &c (7) After treading with almost religious adoration on this classic ground we c^d not leave Stratford without many reflections on &c &c—NB. Avon is there a poor little muddy stream, which w^d have forever remained inglorious, if this Swan had not warbled on its banks— little gabbards with coals & groceries &c come up here from Bristol

Dr Campbell's Diary

FEBRY 28TH   we set off from Shipton by Chappel-
house & breakfasted at Woodstock.—The greatest part
of which road is through a cold clay highly cultivated,
in the broad ridges, but very thin of trees; as most of the
corn grounds I passed through are. For Cheshire &
Shropshire are rather pasturage. The parts about Chappel
house were extremely coarse & hilly.—But Woodstock,
once so famous for the bower of Rosamond, presented us
with a new scene, the most beautiful I ever beheld, the
park of Blenheim!—For this, & the University, at which
we arrived about 12 oclock vid. the Oxford guide—
NB. we went to the Coffee house in the evening where
almost all the Gownsmen we saw were tipsy, & the
streets reechoed with bacchanalian crys as we returned
from Supper with Mr. Barnard (8)—The next night also
we went to another Coffee house & there the scene was
only shifted—all muzzy. This happily abated my enthusiasm conceived for an Oxford education; for such
was the venerability of the place that after taking a
cursory view of it I was almost in a paroxism of superstition—

Oxfordshire seems but a wettish country highly cultivated—& not very thickly planted, it being mostly
corn grounds—but uncultivated commons evince what
the native state of the country is, for they were all either
heath or rushes—The first of March at Oxford was
extremely cold—the rain came on in the evening, & it
was raining at six next morning, but the day turned out
a fine one which made the road to London very pleasant
& nothing c^d be finer than Berkeshire—along this
road we saw Genl Conways, Ld Harcourts, (9) Clifton,

Dr Campbell's Diary

Windsor &c   From Brentford to London is almost all city such as the bad parts of Dublin. on the 2^d of March Covent Garden Play house rec^d me,(10) so that in one week from leaving Dublin I had seen a syllabus of all England.

A gownsman of Oxford thus painted the fellows of All Souls—They lived so luxuriously & indolently that they did nothing but clean their teeth all the morning & pick them all the evening.

FRIDAY 3^d it hailed more than once in the forenoon & it rained almost all the afternoon, so that the streets were very slobbery—The atmosphere over London is above measure heavy, impregnated so strongly with coal that the lower part of St. Pauls & the other churches are blackened prodigiously—

on this day I called on Jack Day(11)—who said so many good things that I asked him why he had not wrote a Comedy—He told me that Kelly(12) owns himself his debtor for several bon mots in his—

Talking of the edacity of the English he said that the stomach of the Irish went & came—but that of the English came & stayed—He complained however that he had got a diarrhea of the tongue

SATURDAY THE 4TH   it rained almost all day—NB. That day I left the Hummums(13) & took a lodging at the Grecian Coffee house(14)—where, after coming from Drury lane, I heard a fellow imitate the black bird, thrush, lark & canary birds so exactly that had I heard the same sounds at proper times & places I sh^d never have suspected them to be any other than original—He also did equally well the mewing & caterwawling of cats, barking of Dogs, & Dogs hunting Cats &c—

Braganza went off well—the poetry is happy enough & the Catastrophe is striking. (15) After the representation of this play a scene ensued which strongly marked the English character—It was the tenth night of the play & it seems that custom hath decided that after the nineth night the prologue & epilogue sh⁴ be discontinued. Neither was announced in the bills—However when the players came on the prologue was called for, & Mr. Palmer—a very handsome mouthing blockhead—answered the call.—When the overture for the farce began to be played the Epilogue was called for—the musick ceased for it could not be heared—a long interval ensued—the players came on—they stood their ground for a long time—but were hissed at length off— Mr. Vernon attempted to speak, but he w⁴ not be heared—still the cry was off, off, the epilogue, &c—after a long pause the bell rang for the musick—this set the house in an uproar—the women however who were singers came on in hopes of charming these savage beasts—but they were a second time pelted off—then Weston—a mighty favourite of the town came on—he was pelted oranges—however he stuck to the stage as if he had vegetated on the spot, & only looked at the gallery & pointed up at it when the orange fell, as if to say I know you that threw that—Once he took up an orange as if in thankfulness & put it in his pocket—this & a thousand other humorous tricks he played yet all to no purpose—John Bull roared on—& poor Weston c⁴ not prevail. The Players came again & again & Vernon

44

after a third effort was allowed to tell the pit that Mrs. Yates was sent for & begged leave that the farce might go on till she came—But this was denied—the house grew more & more clamourous calling for Garrick or Mrs. Yates—at length Mr. Yates comes on & tho' he declared in the most solemn manner that his wife was gone sick to bed, yet this w^d not tame the savages of the gallery—The players were twice hissed off after this till a promise of Mrs. Yates's appearance on Monday &c somewhat abated their madness.—But what to me seemed most expressive of Angloism was the conduct of some in the pit beside me—some were more moderate & asked others why they made such a noise—one before asked another behind, how he dared make such a noise & told him—after some altercation—that he deserved to be turned out of the pit—This produced no other effect but to make my friend behind me more vociferous.—The smallest fraction of such language w^d have produced a duel in the Dublin Theatres—And the millioneth part of the submissions made by these poor players w^d have appeased an Irish audience—yea if they have murdered their fathers—(16)

SUNDAY THE 5TH   I breakfasted with Mr Peirson (Figtree court Middle Temple) (17) & went with him to the Temple Church, a most beautiful Gothic structure— The service was ill read & the singing not according to the rubrick, for it was immediately after the 2^d lesson— The sermon was preached by the Master of the society (18) a brother to Thurloe the atorny General—The discourse was the most meagre composition, (on our Saviours temptation) & the delivery worse—He stood, like Gulliver stuck in the marrow bone, (19) with the sermon, (newspaper like) in his hand, and without grace or emphasis he in slow cadence measured it forth.—In the evening I strolled to Westminster Abby, where I (being locked in) was obliged to listen to a discourse still duller & as ill delivered.

as I love to speculatise upon human nature I cannot help setting down, lest I sh^d forget it, an anecdote I heared this day from my fellow-traveller G———(20) which I sh^d never have heared had he met the reception he expected from the paymaster, his uncle the Provosts (21) quondam friend—He told me that soon after Lord Townsends appointment to the government of Ireland Rigby (22) came over to tamper with his Irish friends to oppose poor Sancho's administration—among the rest he attacked the Provost, from whom he expected no resistance. But the P. having made his terms with Townsend told him that had he applyed earlyer his gratitude to the Duke of B. (23) w^d have made him his obedient creature, but that now his honour was pawned to T—& that he c^d not think of forfeiting that—Rigby went so far as to tell him he c^d not expect to meet the reception he formerly found from his old friends at Bloomsbury—The Provost's answer was that he had a remedy for that in not going *in futuro* to England—R—y then said I have gone too far &c but he stayed in Ireland but another day—soon after, things took another turn i.e. the Bloomsbury faction come into play—The Provost then received a letter from Rigby applauding his propriety of conduct & solliciting his support of Lord Townsends administration.—What a creature is man!

Dr Campbell's Diary

G—— told me that the grand hold the Provost got of Rigbys esteem was this—R—— was distressed in the first career of ambition for money—his credit was low on this side the water—he therefore wrote to the Provost to raise him three thousand pounds as soon as possible.— The Provost sent him bills for the mony the very next week—This by some months outran so far the other's expectation (who looked on Andrews as a man of expense) that it created that attachment which lasted till his death—& which was I presume price of the Provost-ship—NB. at the hour of one there came on a violent shower of hail, while we were in the Temple Church —which was succeeded by heavy rains which lasted till near four—the morning haizy & the evening like-wise—

MARCH THE 6TH   a haizy morning & a drizzling rain at noon—This day (without seeking it) I saw the King in his chair coming from Buckingham house to the Palace of St. James—I sh^d have known him from his picture if I had seen him in Siberia

THE 7TH   I went to see Garrick in Lusignan (24)—The house was full by five—tho' David appears but in one act—This day was a good one, yet not absolutely without rain—I saw the king and queen return from an airing in Hyde park (25)

THE 8TH   it rained hard from 9 till 2 oclock—I this day spent in stroling thro' the town—paid a visit to Tom Orr in the morning, & after dining alone at Dollys (26) I went to the Print Auction at the Piazza Covent Garden; (27) where I was taken in for 1–9–6, for

a book of 80 old heads, & six loose prints—and I deserved it for not going to view them by daylight—for
I took them to be all new &c &c—however they are
worth the mony, for they w^d sell for double the sum in
single prints

9 т н—A wet morning but clear'd up in the middle of
the day, but again it rained hard at night—I dined this
day with my friend S———t, (28) whose wife is I think the
ugliest woman I ever beheld & at least three score—
There dined with us two old maids, her contemporarys,
the sad emblems of a single life—& a rich Cit talking
vulgar nonsense before dinner, & falling asleep after it.—
But in the evening I was fully compensated for this woful
set, by the company of a blind man—Stanly—the leader
of the Oratorio band in Drury lane. (29) This was a very
agreeable person & comely for a blind man. He sat
down to cards after Tea & played with as much ease &
quickness as any man I ever saw. He had the cards
however marked by pricks of a pin. I c^d not from my
cursory examination make the key, whereby he marked
them.—a very stormy night now near eleven—so that
we have not had 24 hours together fair since I came to
London

10 т н Showery from morn to night—this day I went
with my good friend Pierson, & (with Gamble) visited
his agreeable sister Sukey—then went to the Museum (30)
& engaged for Monday next at nine oclock—visited
Christie's picture auction Pallmall (31)—dined at Lowes
Hotel Covent garden, & went to the Oratorio of Judas
Macabaeus (32) to see the King & Queen—and there I for

the first time fell asleep, except in bed, since I came to London.

11TH   It rained incessantly from the hour I awoke i.e. 8 till near 12 that I went to bed, & how much farther that night I know not—This day I dined with the Club at the British Coffee (33)—introduced by my old College friend Day—The president was a Scotch member of parlement—Mayne (34)—& the prevalent interest Scottish—they did nothing but praise Macphersons new history, (35) & decry Johnston (36) & Burke—Day humorously gave mony to the waiter to bring him Johnsons *Taxation no Tyranny* (37)—one of them desired him to save himself the expense for that he sh^d have it from him & glad that he w^d take it away as it was worse than nothing—another said it was written in Johnson's manner but worse than usual for that there was nothing new in it &c &c   The president swore that Burke was gone mad & to prove it adduced this instance—that when the house was obliged the day or two before to call him to order he got up again & foaming like a *play-actor* he said in the words of the Psalmist, *I held my tongue even from good words but it was pain & grief to me;—then I said in my heart that they were all lyars.* (38).

My friend Day however told some storys which turned the Scotch into ridicule—they did however laugh —& irritated the president more than once by laughing at his accent—but he had a good blow at one (who valued himself vastly on his classical knowledge) who describing the device on a Snuff box pointed out a satyr blowing his concha—this raised a loud laugh which made the virtuoso look very silly

Dr Campbell's Diary

12 T H—fair in the morning but the evening varyed with storm, hail & rain—This day I went to Church in the foundling hospital (39) & dined with Mr Scott who is a Governor (40)—I hoped to hear the Charity girl who performed on Friday at the Oratorio but the distance was so great I could not distinguish her voice—Here preached a gentleman who certainly had made elocution his study —but affectation was so visible that he was disgusting— his language poor, his matter borrowed from common place—talking with Scott and Peirson they agreed that the lighting of the city lamps cost £2000 a night—& that the very paving of Oxford Street cost 40000 £ forty thousand (41) but in the latter case they were misinformed —for Mr Combe (42) who was concerned told me it had not cost quite twenty thousand; but as to the lamps they spoke partly from knowledge & partly from calculation

13 T H—rain in the morning but turned out a fair day— This day I walked with Mr Scott down the Blackfriars road (43) as far as the oblisk to see the *future* city from thence &c on my return I saw Viny the Timber vender (44) a very curious man who with great courtesy explained every thing to us—I regreted that I did not know more of wheel carriages &c—however the little I did recollect made Viny profess that he w^d do any thing to satisfy me &c—I bespoke a saddle from his maker Clarke upon his construction &c &c I then dined at the crown & anchor in Sussex Street where we were charged 3–10 for a pound of cod &c—It is amazing the passion our Coun- trymen have for appearing great in London—This very learned gentleman Doctor Jackson (45) methought affected a consequence from calling for shrimp sauce &c while the

Waiter (I saw) was laughing at him for his brogue & appearance—I verily believe that if a Coleraine man was to come here he w^d bespeak nothing but Salmon, merely because it is the most expensive fish in London; though he has it at home for less than a farthing a pound

14. The first entire fair day since I came to London—this day I called at Mr Thrayles where I was rec^d with all respect by M^r & Mr^s Thrail   She is a very learned Lady (46) & joyns to the charms of her own sex the manly understanding of ours:—The immensity of the Brewery astonished me—one large house contains & cannot contain more only four store vessels; each of which contains 1500 barrels & in one of which 100 persons have dined with ease (47)—there are beside in other houses 36 of the same construction but of one half the contents—The reason assigned me that Porter is lighter on the stomach than other beer is that it ferments much more & is by that means more spiritualised—I was half suffocated by letting in my nose over the working floor—for I cannot call it vessel—its area was much greater than many Irish castles.—

Dined alone—having refused an invitation from Mr Boyd (48)—in order to see Garrick. And I saw him—which I could not have done if I had stayed half an hour longer; the pitt being full at the first rush—nor was I disappointed in my expectations, tho' I cannot say he came up to what I had hear'd of him.—But all things appear worse for being forestalled by praises—His voice is husky & his person not near so elegant as either Dodds or Kings—but then his look, his eye is very superior.

Leon however was not I think a character wherein he
c^d display himself. (49)—King's Copper Captain was
nothing like Brown's—yet he was very well in it

15 T H—a fair day—dined with A. D. Congreve. (50)
To whom Dr S. Johnston was Shoolfellow at Litchfield.
The Doctor had visited the A. D. yesterday, by which
accident I learned this circumstance *—The Doctor was
son to a Bookseller at Litchfield—NB. Westminster
round St John's Church is generally but two storys high
—very poor-like & deserted. It seems more wretched
than the worst parts of Dublin—yet I have heard an
Englishman in Dublin say—that the worst parts of
London equalled the best of Dublin—In the Evening I
went with Dr Sims (51) to hear Collins lecture upon
Oratory at the Devil Tavern. (52) And the fellow dis-
played good enunciation & good sense—His ridicule of
the Scots, Welsh & Irish was passing well—Tho' all his
observations were from common place yet the manner
they were delivered gave them weight—Speaking of the
preacher who decrys action in the pulpit—I have shewn
the sad effects of emphasis misplaced—are we therefore
to use no emphasis? and are we not to use action, because
action (as I have shewn) may become monstrous?—But
certainly action is dumb language, else the dumb c^d not
render themselves intelligible; nor c^d pictures speak.
This by the way was not the Lecturers observation but
——————— consequently they who slight just action de-
prive themselves of half the force of expression, & that
too perhaps the most valuable—for the language of
words is artificial, of action natural: & therefore the
latter is universal while the former is only particular

Dr Campbell's Diary

16TH—a fair day—dined with Mr Thrale along with Dr Johnson & Baretti.—Baretti is a plain sensible man, who seems to know the world well. He talked to me of the invitation given him by the College of Dublin, (53) but said it (£100 a year & rooms) was by no means worth his acceptance; & if it had, he said, in point of profit still he would not have accepted it, for that now he could not live out of London. He had returned a few years ago to his own country, but he could not enjoy it & was obliged to return to London to those connections he had been making for near 30 years past. He told me he had several familys with whom both in town & country he c^d go at any time & spend a month. He is at this time on these terms at Mr. Thrale's. And he knows how to keep his ground.—Talking as we all were at Tea of the magnitude of the Beer vessels—he said there was one thing in Mr Thrale's house still more extraordinary —meaning his wife. She gulped the pill very prettily— So much for Barretti! Johnson you are the very man Lord Chesterfield describes. A Hottentot indeed. (54) And tho' your abilities are respectable, you never can be respected yourself. He has the aspect of an Idiot— without the faintest ray of sense gleaming from any one feature. With the most awkard garb & unpowdered grey wig on one side only of his head, he is forever dancing the Devils jig, & sometimes he makes the most driveling effort to whistle some thought in his absent paroxisms. (55) He came up to me & took me by the hand—then sat down on a sofa, & mumbled out that he had hear'd two papers had appeared against him in the course of this week—one of which was that he was to go to Ireland next Summer in order to abuse the hospitality of that

writings. Was this like a man insensible to glory? Thrale then asked him if he had got Miss Reynolds's opinion— for she it seems is a politician—as to that quoth the Doctor it is no great matter, for she could not tell, after she had read it, on which side of the question Mr Burke's speech was. (61)—NB. We had a great deal of conversation about A. D. Congreve—who was his class-fellow at Litchfield School. He talked of him as a man of great coldness of mind, who c^d be two years in London without letting him know it, till a few weeks ago, & then apologizing by saying that he did not know where to enquire for him. (62) This plainly raised his indignation, for he swelled to think that his celebrity sh^d not be notorious to every porter in the street. The A. Deacon, he told me, has a sermon upon the nature of moral good & evil preparing for the press & sh^d he die before publication he leaves 50 £ for that purpose—He said he read some of it to him, but that as he had interrupted him to make some remarks, he hopes never to be troubled with another rehearsal.

17 T H   Patricks day *fair*. Nothing remarkable occurred this day—dined with Tom Orr—where I met Lisson & other Hibernians. Except the Duke of Leinster, charmen & beggars I saw very few people wear Shamrougs—This night I for the first time played Loo—& came off a winner—

18 T H   showry in the forenoon & rainy in the afternoon, & now it is pouring at 11 o'clock—In the morning I went to the Tower alone where I had a contest with one of the redcoats, who led me round. At first he blustered & talked of taking me to the constable of the

Tower—but upon my insisting to go there his crest fell, & he was fain to forego his exaction. This I did merely to try the humour of the people—But people are the same every where—individuals & customs & institutions differ —This night I went to Covent Garden, where maugre Mrs Barrys excellencys, Edward & Eleonora (63) went off insipidly.—I bought an onyx cameo ring, the device a Madona's head & the face (happily) white, the rest of a cornelian colour—price two guineas & two shillings

19 TH. Haizy all day interspersed with showers— Breakfasted with Pierson & took from him a Box ticket for Miss Youngs benefit on Tuesday night (64) a place to be kept &c—I went to St James's, & saw the K & Q go to Chappel. There was more pomp than I expected, for among other errors I had imbibed in Ireland this was one, that the Ld Lieutenant in Ireland appeared always in greater display of state than his Majesty. But the thing is impossible. for I think the Battleax guards is all the apparatus of state in Ireland but the men here, dressed in the same uniform with them,—whose denomination I forgit—are more numerous than them, & besides the yeomen of the guards, & gentlemen pensioners who line all the avenues from the presence chamber to the chappel are more richly dressed than common officers—not to say any thing of the nobility in office, maids of honour &c—Dined with Ld Dartrey, who lives a l'Anglois or rather Francois—the cloth not being at all removed &c—There was the celebrated Mrs Carter, (65) whom I sh^d not have suspected to be either an authoress or an old maid. For she was an unaffected plain well looking woman. yet they told me

she has translated Epictetus & that her Poems are
beautiful—There was also Miss Duckworth who does
not accompany Lady Dartrey to Ireland in May &c—
Coming home I steped into St. James's church where I
saw a grave Gentleman Mr. Parker (66) reading a lecture
on the Catechism out of a book—but whether printed or
not I c.ᵈ not decide—He warned his hearers that the
quantity of Gods grace communicated did not depend on
the quantity of water, wherewith the child was be-
sprinkled, for that it was originally immersion, which
custom was changed in cold climates &c with other wise
saws to the like effect—There were about a hundred
hearers thinly scattered, & there seemed not one for each
candle, & indeed I wonder how anybody stayed in the
Church—I next stepped in to St Martins, in the Strand
which I saw lighted up, but I c.ᵈ get no farther than the
door; such a crowd I never saw under one roof. And
wherefore this—Why there was one Harrison (67) (as I
learned) in the pulpit who was the very reverse of the
other—No bombast-player in Tom Thumb or Chronon-
hoton (68) &c ever so roared & so bellowed as he did—
& his matter was as lifeless as his manner was Hyper-
tragic—A man at the door from whom I learned his name
&c told me he was a very good liver & a fine preacher,
if he had not those ways with him. Yet here the poor
fellow was deceived, for it was those ways (as he called
it) which made him pass for a fine preacher. And this
is a strong example, what action in the pulpit can
atchieve. When action is blamed, it is incongruous action.
For just action is the language of nature. Nothing is
worse than false emphasis, yet are we not to use
emphasis?

Dr Campbell's Diary

20TH—A tolerable day but showry Walked with Pierson over a great part of the city, which I had not seen viz. Moorfields & Barthelomews & Christs Hospital, Bethlehem &c Went in the evening to the Suspicious Husband (69)—Woodward (for whose benefit it was)—holds out wonderfully, he acts with as much spirit as ever, but his looks grow too old for Ranger— The cataract in the entertainment of the Druids was amazingly fine—It was done I suppose by means of a wheel—The perspective too of the Piazza Covent Garden was excellent

21—a sweet soft & fair day—Strolled into the Chapter Coffeehouse, (70) Ave Mary lane, which I had heared was remarkable for a large collection of books, & a reading Society &c—I subscribed a shilling for the right of a years reading, & found all the new publications I sought, & I believe what I am told that all the new books are laid in—some of which to be sure may be lost or mislayed.—Here I saw a specimen of English freedom viz. a whitesmith in his apron & some of his saws under his arm, came in, sat down & called for his glass of punch & the paper, both which he used with as much ease as a Lord. Such a man in Ireland (& I suppose France too or almost any other country) w^d not have shewn himself with his hat on, nor any way unless sent for by some gentleman. Now really every other person in the room was well dressed.—

Pierson dined with me at the Grecian & we went together to the play & tho' both dressed we walked, (71) for here it is not indecorous, as in Dublin, to wear a hat in the boxes. The play was Timanthes, (72) very heavy,

except the last act—Smyth is a mere ape of Barry—
Palmer a fine figure & strong voice & if he had an atom
of judgment w^d be an actor, but he is a wretched,
mouthing ranter.—The farce was the Irish Widow (73)—
Mrs Grevill was not equal to Mrs Sparks & Dodd in
Kecksy was nothing to Ryder. Slingsby (74) danced, after
the play, the provencalle dance with Sig^a Hidou &
admirably he did dance—Between the acts of the farce
was introduced a dance called the *Irish fair*: Into which
were introduced several Irish tunes—a hornpipe was
danced to Kin-du-deelas (75)—a Drum was introduced on
the Stage to give it hub-bub air—but it w^d have still been
better (tho' it was very well) if they had introduced the
bagpipe also. As Slingsby was so excellent the Irishry
of tonight went off well. Though I dont think the farce
hit the English taste. Either I am mistaken or the best
of the English dont think as ill of the Irish as I expected—

Let me not forget to set down what Ryland, (76) who
is now one of the first engravers, told me—what indeed
I had always heard in Ireland—that old West was the
best drawer in red chalks at Paris of his time & that for
drawing in general he was the best scholar of Venloo.—
I remember Dixon at Wests academy, whose drawing,
he says is better than any other mettzotincto scraper's—
Burke is his scholar, & he is now among the first—So
that all the Scrapers have been Irish except one; *Earlom!*
M'ardell was the first of his time then Fry, now Watson,
Fisher Dixon Burke &c quere—

22. a fair day—nothing remarkable—

23 D. fair also, but rain at night—dined at the Bedford, where I met Doctor Jackson—lamenting the state

of his wife from the case of the Perreaus (77) her brothers
—I went to Ranelagh (78) where there were few Ladies
except of pleasure—The room beautiful & about four
times the size of the Rotunda (79)—But Almack's (80)
rooms are by far the finest I have yet seen. The ball
room is above 90 by 40—the serpentine wreaths round
the pillars was prettyly painted, & every thing finished
in the best manner—The tables were laid out in the
rooms under this for supper—The display for the Dessert
was sumptuous & in short every thing in the most elegant
style—Called on Lord Dacre for Fombell's (81) papers—
He asked me to dine &c—I find the first method of
conciliating an Englishman is to praise England.

24 T H   a fair day—called on Mr Combe with Dean
W's (82) letter—he rec.^{d} me with great courtesy &c called
also at Dr Campbells (83) but found him not at home—
Dined from mere curiosity at a shilling ordinary in the
Strand, where I own I was better pleased at the ad-
venture—for such I call it—than any thing I saw in
London yet. For it exhibited a view of people who
affected somewhat above themselves, better than any
thing I have seen in real life. The company was mostly
Scotch, & they called each other, Colonel, or Captain or
Doctor. There were two or three cocheads [?] (84) & an
old highland parson who, being much of his life abroad,
had almost forgot the Erse & had not learned much
English—They talked high of Lords & Ladys & their
engagements with them &c &c

25 T H.   Eddying winds in the forenoon rendered the
streets very disagreeable with dust, which was layed in
the evening by rain from 3 &c—Dined at Mr Thrales,

Dr Campbell's Diary

where there were 10 or dz gentlemen & but one lady
besides Mrs Thrale. The dinner was excellent, first course
soups at head & foot removed by fish & a saddle of
mutton—second course a fowl they called Galena (85)—
at head, & a capon—larger than some of our Irish
turkeys—at foot—Third course four different sorts of
Ices viz. Pineapple, Grape, rasberry & a fourth—in
each remove there were I think fourteen dishes—The
two first courses were served in massy plate. I sat
beside Barretti which was to me the richest part of the
entertainment. He & Mr & Mrs Thrale joynd in expressing to me Dr Johnston's concern that he could not
give me the meeting that day, but desired that I sh^d go
& see him &c &c—Barretti was very humorous about
his new publication, which he expects to put out next
month. (86) He there introduces a dialogue about Ossian
&c wherein he ridicules the Idea of its double translation
into Italian &c &c in hopes—as he said—of having it
abused by the Scots. Which w^d give it an imprimature
for a second edition; & he had stipulated for 25 guineas
additional if the first sh^d sell in a given time. (87)—He
repeated to me (upon memory) the substance of the
letters which passed between Dr Johnson & Mr. Mc-
Pherson. (88) The latter tells the Doctor that neither his
age nor infirmitys sh^d protect him, if he came in his way
&c—The Doctor responds that no menaces of any rascal
sh^d intimidate him from detecting imposture wherever
he met it

26TH rain in the morning, hail about one, rain at
three &c & a copious fall of snow at night—This day
was the first on which I heared good preaching in

61

Dr Campbell's Diary

England—and indeed Mr. Warner (89) has in my sight redeemed the honour of his nation, for he is positively the best deliverer of a discourse I ever hear'd. He is the very thing I have often conceived a preacher ought to be, & his manner is what I sh^d have aimed at had it been my lot to be a preacher in any great city. He does not (as he ought not) to rely on his notes—He makes excursions & unwritten effusions, which prevail over the warmest the boldest compositions & then when he hath exhausted such sentiments as present themselves he returns to his notes, & takes up the next head according to his preconceived arrangement. By this discreet conduct he avoids the frozen beaten track of declamation, & keeps clear of the labyrinth of nonsense into which those enthusiasts wander, whose vanity or hypocracy rejects the clue of composition.—This day furnished me with a new fact. I learned that (according to the custom of London) any person may build a chappel & by licence of the Bishop, preach & pray in it publickly. &c—This Mr Warner has done & his income arises from renting the seats. This house—called Tavistock chappel—must bring a goodly revenue, for it is capacious—of the square figure—& well filled. Indeed it ever must be so while its pulpit is so well filled.

Dined this day with Mr Combe who is an easy sensible man—his daughters are not to be as handsome as either father or mother tho' like both—the eldest taller than her mother—I saw 3 Girls & 2 boys—these are young— This I set down lest I sh^d forget it, before I see Mrs Woodward & the Dean &c—NB. I since hear that Warner has sold this chappel for 4500—so these shops

for preaching are bought & sold like other warehouses—
or Theatres &c—NB. M.ʳ Combe told me from his own
knowledge that the paving of Oxford Street came but to
between 19 & 20000 £ for it is current in London that
it cost forty thousand

27 ᴛ ʜ   Frost in the morning & light falls of snow all
day—Went to see Reynolds's pictures—His manner is
certainly the true sublime—the colours seem laid on so
coarsely that *quivis speret idem.* (90) Gainsboroughs I
looked at afterward—but his work seems laboured with
small pencils. I dont think he paints as well as Hunter in
Dublin—What a pity that Reynolds colours do not
stand—they want a body, they seem glazed

Went to the Pantheon (91) in the evening it is a
beautiful room & highly finished, with colums—of post
—resembling porphyry—or Armagh marble rather—But
after all the orchestra seemed by no means of a piece &
awkardly disposed—the cercular are not so large as the
Rotunda, but with the Piazza it holds more—beside the
gallery & great tea room below—equal to the whole
area above, & besides the several rooms off it—There
was the Prussian Ambassador (92)—a white-faced white-
haired, northern-like man—he had nothing of sensibility
in his countenance—Lord Stormont (no very sage-looking
man) was there & several Stars—The Duke of Cumberland & Lady Grovernor—a fine woman lost to all sense
of modesty—met over & over & looked away from each
other (93)—L.ᵈ Littleton a mean looking person, but of
no mean understanding—Lady Archer—painted like a
Doll, but handsome, her feathers nodded like the plumes
of Mambrinos helmet (94)—yet some of the whores had

longer—peacock-feathers. (95) There seem to be fewer
ugly women among the English than the Irish but I
cannot say there are more handsome—Lady Townshend
was by most people reckoned the handsomest woman
there. But if Lady Grosvenor (96) was modest & her
complexion natural she w^d be my beauty—They say she
has poxed Ld Hinchinbrooke—The singing by the Italian
woman (who is handsome & of expressive gesticulation.)
was beyond any thing I c^d conceive in the compass of a
voice—Garrick was there & by no means that well
limbed man I have heared him cryed up for, but his eye
is excillence

NB. I forgot to set down an article of the day I dined
last at Thrales. Barretti complained that Major Vallancy
had treated him ill in his discourse on the antiquity of
the Irish language &c—by saying that he had misrepre-
sented the copy he gave of Biscayan Paternoster—for
says he I quote one,—he quotes another & a fifth might
be quoted all different from each other. Now says he I
could not misrepresent for I did not understand—& the
fact is I did not misrepresent, for I can produce the book
from whence I quoted (97)

28 T H—The coldest day I felt this season, rain, hail,
snow & sleet—Dined with Ld Dacre—& I cannot help
remarking how similar all the great dinners I have met
with are—the soup, fish & saddle of mutton—turkey &
pidjeons & second course—Ices & fruits dessert—He
affects knowledge particularly of antiquity (98)—Here
dined the man I conjecture from whom Foote drew his
Cadwallader—If he is not the original he certainly is like
Foote's Cadwallader—his name is something like

Cousbel or &c (99)—NB. The two Ropers (100) & the wife to one of them—a pint of claret I think was not consumed—Here as almost every where else in England I found a strong partiality in favour of their own Country —The intense coldness of the day gave occasion to talk of the weather—& it was agreed that Paris had some-times as bad—a Lady bridling herself said every one allows that we have every thing better than the French except climate—& I who have spent much of my time in Paris think that we have even a better climate (101)—

A few days ago in a large company it was argued that Englishmen had no right to talk so loud in favour of liberty, as they enslaved without mercy the blacks &c abroad—a young man in a passion exclamed that God almighty had made them slaves, for they were black, flat-nosed & negros—& then concluded with *Old England forever!*

29TH Intensely cold—the streets were white with snow about 12 o'clock—which soon melted—& the snow came on again at five—NB. Leoni for which I p^d 2–5–6 is but 1–7–0 in the catalogue here (102)—

30TH Colder if possible—Hail & snow showers all day i.e. at intervals—Dined at the Grecian with Mr Rose of Dublin, & went with him to Covent Garden to see the Barrys in the Grecian Daughter, (103) but c^d not get seats a little after 5—so I went to the two shilling gallery in Drury lane & saw the Distressed Mother (104) most dis-tressingly performed for the benefit of Slingsby—whose Tambourine Dance made some amends—& King in the peep from behind the curtain was excellent; not that the composition was so, but there was something ridiculous enough in Orpheus lulling Euridice to sleep, & in his setting men cows sheep &c &c a dancing—Miss Younge was very poor in Hermione, perhaps she w^d not have appeared so if had not seen Mrs Fitzhenry—and the creature who did Andromache was not fit to be a Scullion in Hectors kitchen

31—Fair but cold—I read the answer to *Taxation no Tyranny.* (105) It reprobates Johnsons position of the supremacy of even the legislature forasmuch as all power originates in the people & is only delegated to a few for the good of the whole. This is the limit of their power. And whenever that is overleaped, the supremacy reverts to the people, they are *ipso facto* invested with the right of resistance. For w^d it not be absurd to suppose that fourteen millions of people sh^d be a sacrifice to one thousand?—The parallel too between the American assemblys & the parish vestrys doth not apply, for many reasons, but principally for this—that the assemblys cannot of themselves legislate; the concurrence of the crown is necessary. But with this consent an act of assembly becomes a law binding upon that province. But this is not the case with a vestry.—The distinction of actual & virtual representation is sophistical; for representation is a right appendant not to persons but things, i.e. property—so that American property can neither be actually nor virtually represented in a British parlement—Besides there is this to be said for a British parlement taxing all the people of Britain, whether represented or not—the commons lay no greater burdens upon the shoulders of others than on their own. They pay every tax in common with every other subject—Whereas

memory—Boswell arguing in favour of a chearful glass
adduced the maxim *in vino veritas*—well, says Johnson,
& what then unless a man has lived a lye.—B. then urged
that it made a man forget all his cares—That to be sure,
says Johnson, might be of use if a man sat by such a
person as *you*. (109)—Boswell confessed that he liked a
glass of whiskey in the Highland tour & used to take it—
at length says Johnson let me try *wherein the pleasure of a
Scotsman consists*, & so tips off a brimmer of whiskey. (110)
—But Johnsons abstemiousness is new to him, for within
a few years he w^d swallow two bottles of port without
any apparent alteration,—& once in the company with
whom I dined this day he say'd—pray Mr Thrale give
us another bottle. (111)—It is ridiculous to pry so nearly
into the movements of such men—yet Boswell carrys it
to a degree of superstition. The Doctor is seems has a
custom of putting the peel of oranges into his pocket &
he asked the Doctor what use he made of them—the
Doctors reply was, that his dearest friend sh^d not know
that. (112)—This has made poor Boswell unhappy, & I
verily think he is as anxious to know the secret as a green
sick girl &c—NB. The book wherewith Johnson presented the highland lady was Cocker's Arithmetick (113)
—Murphy gave it (on Garricks authority) that when it
was asked what was the greatest pleasure, Johnson
answered f—g & the second was drinking. And therefore he wondered why there were not more drunkards,
for all could drink tho' all could not f—k. But Garrick
is his most intimate friend—They came to London
together—& he is very correct both in his conduct &
language.—As a proof of this they all agreed in a story
of him & Dr James, (who is it seems a very lewd fellow

both *verbo & facto*,) James, it seems, in a coach with his whoor, took up Johnson & set him down at a given place—Johnson hearing afterward what the lady was, attacked James, where next he met him, for carrying him about in such company—James apologized by saying that he always took a swelling in his stones if he abstained a month &c—Damn the rascal says Johnson, he is past sixty the swelling wᵈ have gone no farther (114).—

Boswell desirous of setting his native country off to the best advantage expatiated upon the beauty of a certain prospect, particularly, upon a view of the sea. O Sir, says Johnson, *the sea is the same everywhere.* (115)

NB. Murphy does not understand Greek—for talking of Goldsmith's Vicar of Wakefield, he said that he had ridiculed the moral standard of a fitness of things &c better than Feelding in the person of the villain who in prison & elsewhere supports his opinion by Greek sentences from Epictetus viz. τον δ'απαμειβομενος &c (116)

Dᴿ Johnson calls the act in Braganza (117) with the monk paralytick in one side; i.e. the monc is introduced without any notification of his character & so that any other monk or any other person might as well be introduced in the same place & for the same purpose—And I myself say that Velasquez quitting his hold of the Dutchess, upon sight of the monk is an effect without a sufficient cause. The cool intrepid character of Velasquez required that he shᵈ either have dispatched or attempted to dispatch the monk—& then there wᵈ have been a pretext for losing hold of the Dutchess &c—The Duke is a poor tame animal & by no means equal to his historic character.

Dr Campbell's Diary

A whimsical incident I was witness to there—Murphy told a very comical story of a Schotmans interview with Dr Johnston, upon his earnest desire of being known to the Doctor—&c! This was Boswell himself!(118)

NB. The Tour to the western Isles was written in 20 days—& the Patriot in three. Taxation no Tyranny within a week—& not one of them w^d have yet seen the light had it not been for Mrs Thrale & Barretti, who stirred him up by laying wagers &c

AP. 2D—fair I went to the Chappel Royal & heard the Bishop of Bangor preach—His subject was on these two commandments &c (119)—His object was to prove that piety & virtue went hand in hand & c^d not exist separately—his proofs were taken first from the state of paganism where as the theology was more or less refined, so was their morality more or less pure—& from experience of persons whose virtuous qualitys were generally adequate to their notions of the divinity &c then he shewed the inefficacy of the motives from the fittness of things, or the beauty of virtue &c & so resolved all into the will of God. He touched upon the folly of Enthusiasm & instanced the violence of the Fanaticks in the last century, to impress a sense of the error of religion consisting merely in devotion—then he glanced at the licentious reign which followed—then ended abruptly by saying that this was neither time nor place for discussing that matter &c—NB. The Bp of London (120) read the communion service—but not according to the rubric, for at the *let us pray* after the commandments he did not turn round to the communion table—

Dr Campbell's Diary

In the evening I went to St Martins in hopes of hearing Harrison & the church was very full from the same expectations—but we were all disappointed for Dr Scott (Anti-Sejanus) mounted the pulpit, & as I c^d not well hear him, tho' just behind the pulpit, I went off to St Stephens Wallbrook, not for hearing—for I knew not who was to be there—but of seeing the Church which is reckoned the handsomest in the world.—They tell the following story of it,—that Ld Burlington (who was the patron of architecture &c) saw in Italy a church which he so admired & bepraised that he got drawings made of it as the *chef de oeuvrè* of human skill &c but being told that it was a copy from Sir C. Wren's Wallbrook he c^d not believe it, till he examined it; & what is very remarkable they add that coming late into London he drove there directly & viewed it by candle light. (121)— This is the story in London, but as Sr Christopher stole his plan of St Pauls from St Peters why may it not be expected that the Italian Church is the original & not the copy—It revolts against the *costume* that an Italian Architect would borrow models from London—

NB. Lazarus is a good text for a sermon on the immortality of the soul—forasmuch as the only moral proof of it arises from the sufferings of the good & the enjoyments of the wicked in this life &c—

AP. 3^d Fair—I went to the British Museum—The sight was so various that it is hard to remember anything distinctly.—But what pleased me most was the ruins of Herculaneum.—The original magna charta of K John was in the Harleian I think (122)—The shell for which a cardinal gave 500 £ I w^d be sorry to give five

71

pence for, unless merely because it is a specimen of human folly—The magnitude of the crocodile (20 feet) & the horn (5 feet at least) growing out of the nose of the unicorn fish were extraordinary—to me—The form of the pulpits was curious. A cylindrical form with spiral geometrical stairs issuing from the central upright. This evening I sketched out a letter on the method to read the Liturgy &c (123)

NB. The transparent picture of Vesuvius in the last eruption from the side, done by direction Sir Wm Hamilton was very well

AP. 4. a Drizzling rain from 10 till four—I went to the house of Lords—on the Montague appeal & heard L^{ds} Mansfield, Cambden, & the great Lawyers at the bar &c (124)—This night I finished my address to the Clergy on the liturgy &c

AP. 5. fair—Dined with Dilly in the Poultry, as guest to Mr Boswell (125)—where I met Dr Johnson (—& a Mr. Miller who lives near Bath; who is a Dilettanti man, keeps a weekly day for the litterati, & is himself so litterate that he gathereth all the flowers that Ladys &c write & bindeth into a garland (126)—&c but enough of him) with several others particurly a Mr. Scott (127) who seems to be a very sensible plain man— The Doctor when I came in had an answer titled Taxation Tyranny to his last Pamphlet in his hand—He laughed at it & said he w^d read no more of it for that it payed him compliments but gave him no information.— He asked if there were any more of them. (128) I told him I had seen another, & that the Monthly reveiw had handled it in what, I believed, he called the way of information &c(129)—Well says he I sh^d be glad to see it. Then Boswell (who understands his temper well) asked him somewhat for I was not attending relative to the provincial assemblys. (130) The Doctor, in process of discourse with him, argued with great vehemence, that the assemblys were nothing more than our vestrys &c— I asked him was there not this difference that an act of the assemblys required the kings assent to pass into a law &c His answer had more of wit than argument— Well Sir says he that only gives it more weight— I thought I had gone too far—but dinner was then announced & Dilly who paid all attention to him in placing him next the fire said, (131) Doctor perhaps you will be too warm—No Sir says the Doctor I am neither hot nor cold—and yet, said I, Doctor, you are not a lukewarm man.—This I thought pleased him. And as I sat next him I had a fine opportunity of attending to his Phiz. and I could clearly see he was fond of having his quaint things laughed at; & they (without any force) gratifyed my propensity to affuse grinning.—Mr. Dilly led him to give his opinion of men & things, of which he is very free, & Dilly will probably retail them all. Talking of the Scotch (after Boswell was gone) (132) he said though they were not a learned nation, yet they were far removed from ignorance. Learning was new among them & he doubted not but they w^d in time be a learned people—for they were a fine bold enterprising people. He compared England & Scotland to two Lyons the one saturated with his belly full, & the other prowling for prey.—But the test he offered to prove that Scotland, tho' it had learning enough for common life, yet had not

all he said, (which was not much—but it was) in repro-
bating the measures of the ministry towards the
Americans &c—He then sat down & Capt Allen after
making a speech, too trivial for a mountibank,—yet he
too was applauded—read the address petition & remonstrance—which will be in the prints &c (139)—

Talking of Addisons timidity keeping him down so
that he never spoke in the house of commons was he said
much more blameworthy than if he had attempted &
failed; as a man is more praise worthy who fights & is
beaten than he who runs away. (140)

AP. 6.   Light showers—Dined with Ld Dartry, who
promised to print Swifts letter (141) next week—I went
in the evening to the Italian opera in the Haymarket—for
Sestini's benefit. (142)—An *Italian* opera is not so absurd
an entertainment as I expected—For it is nearly as
intelligible as if it were in English, considering the
inarticlation of the words by the Singers—The grand
absurdity lyes against an opera at large i.e. an attempt
to express the passions by singing. And yet the action
of the Italian performers is so just that their language
of dumb shew w^d be intelligible without the aid of song.
—However this was the first & it shall be the last
sacrifice I shall make of sense to sound.

AP. 7.   Cold in the morning with some rain but turned
out a fine day—I went down to Greenwich & viewed the
Hospital & the outside of Flamsteads observatory—the
inside not being to be seen without some special order,
on account of some thefts committed &c I walked from
thence to Woolwich & viewed the Dock yard particularly, a 74 gun ship, not finished which is truly a mon-

strous vessel—In the Warren, as it is called, I saw a great number of Cannon &c & bombs piled up in huge Pyramids & prisms—large as Irish turf stack—This is a poor place, as I suppose all places must be that depend on letting lodgings &c

The prospect from King Johns palace (as they call it) about midway beween Greenwich & Woolwich was fine, the bow of the river bending in a sweet curve— NB. There were Hawthorn trees in greenwich park almost full in leaf—as they were quite green—There were others however not so forward—apple trees in full blossom

AP. 8. Very cold; & some rain, but not enough to allay the blowing of the dust.—Dined with Thrale where Dr Johnson was & Boswell (& Barretti as usual)(143)— The Doctor was not in as good spirits as he was at Dillys. He had supped the night before with Lady ——(144) Miss Jeffrys one of the maids of honour Sir Ja Reynolds &c at M.rs Abbingtons. He said Sir C. Thompson & some others who were there spoke like people who had seen good company, & so did M.rs Abbington herself— who could not have seen good company.(145)

He seems fond of Boswell, & yet he is always abusing the Scots before him, by way of joke(146)—talking of their nationality—he said they were not singular—The negros & Jews being so too.—Boswell lamented there was no good map of Scotland.—There never can be a good of Scotland, says the Doctor sententiously. This excited Boswell to ask wherefore. Why Sir to measure land a man must go over it; but who c.d think of going over Scotland?(147)

Dr Campbell's Diary

When Dr Goldsmith was mentioned & Dr. Percys intention of writing his life,(148) he expressed his approbation strongly, adding that Goldsmith was the best writer he ever knew upon every subject he wrote upon.

He said that Kendric(149) had borrowed all his Dictionary from him—Why says Boswell every man who writes a dictionary must borrow.—No! Sir says Johnson that is not necessary. Why says Boswell have not you a great deal in common with those who wrote before you—Yes Sir says Johnson I have the words. But my business was not to *make* words but to explain them.

Talking of Garrick & Barry—he s^d he always abused Garrick himself but when any body else did so he fought for the Dog like a Tyger(150)—As to Barry he said he supposed he c^d not read—& how does he get his part says one—Why—some body reads to him. And yet I know says he that he is very much admired. Mrs Thrale then took him by repeating a repartee of Murphy—(The setting Barry up in competition with Garric is what irritates the English Criticks) & Murphy standing up for Barry, Johnson said that he was fit for nothing but to stand at an auction room door with his pole &c— Murphy said that Garrick w^d do the business as well & pick the people's pockets at the same time.—Johnson admitted the fact but said Murphy spoke nonsense for that peoples pockets were not picked at the door, but in the room &c &c(151)—Then say'd I he was worse than the pick pocket, forasmuch as he was Pandar to them— this went off with a laugh—*vive la Bagatelle.*(152) It was a case decided here, that there was no harm & much

pleasure in laughing at our absent friends.—And I own
if the character is not damaged I can see no injury done

A P. 9.   A fair day—went to St Clemts to hear Mr
Burrows, (153) so cryed up by Ld Dartrey, preach.   But I
was wofully disappointed—His matter is cold, his manner
hot, his voice weak, & his action affected.—Indeed I
thought he preached from a printed book—a book it
certainly was; & it seemed at my distance—which was
the perpendicular to the side of the pulpit—to have a
broad marginlike print; & he did not seem master of
it, yet he affected warmth emphasis & action.   Dined
with Mr Combe & spent the Evening with Doctor
Campbell (154)

A P. 10.   Rain—but not enough to soften the asperity
of the weather.—Dined with General Oglethorpe (155)—
who was in lieu of Aid-du-Camp (for he had no such
officer about him) to Prince Eugene, & celebrated by
Mr Pope (156)—Dr Johnson pressed him to write his life
adding that no life in Europe was so well worth recording &c—The old man excused himself saying the
life of a private man was not worthy public notice—He
however desired Boswell to bring him some good
Almanac; that he might recollect dates—& seemed to
excuse himself also on the article of incapacity &c but
Boswell desired him only to furnish the skeleton & that
Dr Johnson would supply Bones & sinews &c (157)—He
wd be *a good Doctor* says the General who wd do that—
Wel, says I he is *a good Doctor.* at which he the Doctor
laughed very heartily.—

Talking of America, it was observed that his works
wd not be admired there &c No! says Boswell we shall

soon hear of his being hung in effigy &c (158) I sh^d be glad of that says the Doctor—that w^d be a new source of fame—alluding to some conversation on the fullness of his fame which had gone before.—And says Boswell, I wonder he has not been hung in effigy from the Hebrides to England &c—I shall suffer them to do it corporeally says the Doctor if they can find me a tree to do it upon (159)—

The Poem of *the Graces* (160) became the topic. Boswell asked if he had ever been under the hands of a dancing master (161)—Ay & a dancing mistress too says the Doctor. But I own to you I never took a lesson but one or two; my blind eyes shewed me I could never make a proficiency.—Boswell led him to give his opinion of Gray. he said there were but two good stanzas in all his works viz. the elegy (162)—Boswell desirous of eliciting his opinion upon too many subjects as he thought, he rose up & took his hat—This was not noticed by any body, as it was nine o clock—but after we got into Mr Langton's coach (who gave us a set down) he said— Boswells conversation consists entirely in asking questions, & it is extremely offensive &c (163)—We defended it upon Boswell's eagerness to hear the Doctor speak &c—

Talking of suicide—Boswell took up its defence for argument sake—& the Doctor said that some cases were more excusable than others but if it were excusable it sh^d be the last resource &c for instance says he if a man is distressed in circumstances (as in the case I mentioned of Denny) he ought to fly his country &c (164)—How can he fly says Boswell if he has wife & children?—What

Sir says the Doctor—shaking his head as if to promote the fermentation of his wit—Doth not a man fly from his wife & children, if he murders himself?—

A P. 11. Fair from ten—bought quilts &c supped with M.ʳ Crawford at the Adelphi; where except a Dr. Wilkinson [?] (165) the company was all Irish, & with the burning zeal of their country violent patriots in their own opinion

A P. 12—Fair—went to Kensington—where the ground is in many places so bad that the trees were stunted & ranpiked (166) as they call it in Ireland—Dined with Mosse (167) & Rose at the exchange coffee house where things were dear & bad

—13—Fair & cold—Went to see the King proceed from St James's to give the royal assent to the restraining bill &c (168) Strolled with Mosse &c

14. Fair—Good Friday—went to hear Dr Dodd, (169) who is cryed up as the first preacher in London, at his own Chappel—He reads better than he preaches—for in the pulpit he leans too much upon his notes—his eyes are seldom off them—yet he mises the action of an extempore delivery, which makes a jaring jumble. His manner however is infinitely superior to his matter— which was a poor & unsuccessful attempt upon the passions—He said the merits of Xt were applyed to us, just as a man's paying a money debt for another was deemed a discharge for the debt—& he said that as the merits of Xt extended from the rising up of the sun to the going down of the same, so they extended equally

Dr Campbell's Diary

a parte ante & post since creation to those who never heard the name—i.e., J. Xt was a vicarious sacrifice as well for those who lived before him as those who have lived since, & as well for those who never hear'd of him as those who have faith in his name—

NB. The Shops were not shut up today, farther than that some of them had a single board standing up—The Paviours went on as all other workmen did—& the Soldiers went to their exercise in Hyde park as usual NB. Dodd did not read the Communion service rubrically for he kneeled at the beginning, & tho it was a fast day he & his coadjutor wore surplices &c—Supped with Jack Day & a set of Irish &c—

AP. 15—Heavy rain till twelve, yet without softening the asperity of the weather—

AP. 16—rain till nine—The weather softer, but boisterous still—Went to hear Harrison at Brompton chappel his discourse incoherent & delivered in the gout of a Spouter—It is ridiculous in these fellows, whose eyes are scarce ever off the book to affect the animation of extemporaneous warmth.—yet this Mans composition inclined to vehemence—Talking of the corruption of the present times he said Xtns professed a creed indeed, but acted as if they had no belief—they offered a public sacrifice as on this day, yet they lived as if they sacrificed to the Devil—His text was Rom. 6–5 (170)—Dined with A. D. Congreve—my Ld Primate (171) came there in evening—He asked me sneeringly if I had seen the Lions (172)—I told him I had neither seen them nor the crown, nor the jewels, nor the whispering gallery at St Pauls &c—The conversation turned upon other things,

& came round to his Picture by Reynolds; which led on talk of Sir Joshua & other great artists. And without any force I introduced something of Johnson &c—What says he do you know him? Yes my Lord I do & Barretti & several others whom I have been fortunate enough to find willing to extend my acquaintance among their friends—for these my Lord were the Lions I came to see in London. Aye, says he, these indeed are lions worth seeing & the sight of them may be of use to you.—He soon after talked to me if my brother were not curate to Dr Bissett (173) &c & whether he was not contemporary with Scott (174)—whom he looked upon he sayed as a friend to the Clergy &c &c—He asked too if some body else had not spoke to him about my brother &c—I mentioned Lᵈ Chief Justice Patterson (175) &c—He spoke in such a way that I take it in my head he will do something for him out of this living of Donaghmore

A P. 17—Showry, yet the air not yet softened—Disappointed of a ticket for the Lᵈ Mayor's ball

18 T H—Went in one of the Brentford coaches to Kew Bridge—walked from thence along the Thames—(NB. a smart shower then)—to Richmond: near which I met the King with a single gentleman & two of the Princes. I did not know him till I was cheek for jowl with him (Jowl here I apply to his majesty)—& then I took off my hat—

Sometime before I met the King I overtook a boy of 15 or 16 dressed in flannel or something of that sort—I asked him several questions; to all which he answered with English curtness—He was however glad of a penny for carrying my coat &c—After passing the King I asked

Dr Campbell's Diary

him if he knew who that was—He answered in the
negative—I then told him that is the King. He shewed
no emotion, but turned round, & said leisurely—is that
the King?—an Irish boy w^d have doged him at the heels
as long as he could—It would be heresy here to deny
that Richmond hill afforded the finest prospect in the
world—& it w^d be false to deny that it afforded a rich
one—yet it has nothing picturesque to be seen from it—
for it wants the 2d & 3d distances—Wales is the fertil
mother of Landscapes.—NB. Richmond hill is very
coarse ground, covered with furz & rushes.

AP. 19TH—Tho it rained heavily last night the cold
nothing abated, but rather increased—Showry in the
forenoon & a most severe fall of hail at two o clock—
dined at Boyds—[In the manuscript some blank places
on this page are filled in with notes for 1776 and 1781.
These will be found later in proper sequence]

AP. 20—fair & somewhat softened by the fall of hail
yesterday &c—Dined at Thrale's with Dr Johnson (176)
Barretti & a Dean Wetherell of Oxford; (177) who is
solliciting for a riding house at Oxford—When I mentioned to the Doctor another answer intitled *Resistance
no Rebellion* (178) coming out—He said that is the seventh.
the author finds the other six will not do—& I foresee
that the Title is the best part of the book—He desired
that I sh^d visit him &c NB. Talking—after dinner—of
the measures he w^d pursue with the Americans (179)—he
said the first thing he w^d do w^d be to quarter the Army
on the Citys & if any refused free quarters, he w^d pull
down that persons house, if it was joyned to other
houses; but w^d burn it if it stood alone—This & other

83   6-2

schemes he proposed in the manuscript copy of *Taxation no Tyranny*—but these he said the Ministry expunged (180)

A P. 21—Fair but cold—Went with Mosse & Weld (181) to Ld Chesterfields & the Duke of Bedfords (182)—There is nothing in the latter worth looking at—but in Ld Chesterfields everything is admirable. That elegance of which his Lordship was so great an advocate & so shining an example pervades the whole. The stair case, noble & of the finest white marble—The rooms highly finished, & rather beautiful than magnificent—The effect of looking glass pannels placed opposite to the windows of the Musick room was admirable—it apparently doubled the real dimension, & gave a sweet reflected view of Stanhope Street & Hyde park—There was a Madona & sleeping Xt from Guido admirable & finely copyed by a Master whom I forget—There was also a good Rubens—The subject Joseph virgin & child—Dined as umbra (183) to Weld & Mosse with a Citizen—but I'll do so no more—for there is no entertainment but meat & drink with that class of people

A P. 22 D—Rainy morning—the air still harsh—showry the rest of the day—went to Cheltsea, & saw the Hospital &c—And tho' I had been at Ranelagh garden I did not know it was at Chelsea &c &c—

23 D—Rainy almost all day—hail & thunder about three at Hampton Court—The Gardens must hurt any delicate feelings, with their semicircular fish pond &c—on the bank of the Thames—The Palace presents two suits of rooms, in which are exhibited a few good pictures (viz. Wm 3. by G. Kneller the Spanish Embassa-

dors &c) among several ordinary things—some choice
Tapestrys viz. the battles of Alexander from Le Brun;
& Diogenes in his tub visited by Alexander from Salvator
Rosa—The Hampton Court Beautys by Kneller &c—

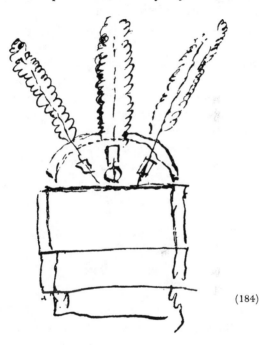

(184)

24—Rainy morning—Sat an hour with Dr Johnson
about noon—He was at breakfast with a Pindar (185) in
his hand—& after saluting me with great cordiality—he
after whistling in his way over Pindar layed the book
down—& then told me he had seen my Ld Primate at
Sir Joshua's, & I believe says I have not recommended
myself much to him—for I differed widely in opinions
from him (186)—yet I hear he is doing good things in

Ireland—I mentioned Skelton (187) to him as a man of strong imagination &c & told him the story of his selling his library for the support of the poor—He seemed much affected by it—& then fell a rowling & muttering to himself—& I could hear him plainly say after several minutes pause from conversation—Skelton is a great good man—He then said I propose reading his Ophio-machis—for I have never seen any thing of his, but some allegoric peices which I thought very well of—He told me he had seen Delany (188) when he was in every sense *gravis annis*—but he was able man says he, his Revelation examined with candour was well received—& I have seen an introductory preface to a second edition of one of his books, which was the finest thing I ever read in the declamatory way—He asked me whether Clayton (189) was an English or Irish man &c—He endeavoured to raise a hissy among you, says he, but without effect I believe—I then told him one effect in the case of the parish clerks &c—His indignation rose prodigiously—Aye says he these are the effects of heretical notions upon vulgar minds

25 T H—Fair & softer—Dined in Nicholas Lane Lombard Street with M.ᵣ Portis, (190) an Irish man who gave plenty of claret—

26—Warm—viewed the Exhibition by the Artists in the Strand (191)—which is far inferior to that by the Royal Academy Pall mall (192) in every thing—Even in land-skips & horses

27—Warm or rather hot, to the degree of astonish-ment with the folks here—Revisited the exhibition of the Royal Academy & am confirmed in my opinion of *the*

grand manner of *Barrys Venus lamenting over Adonis*—
Barrets Landskips had escaped me on Tuesday, but they
are superlative—Ashford copys & rivals Roberts—Dined
at M͞r Weld's—Clements Inn—Where I for the first
time saw Kelly, the Poet &c—obstinately refused to go
with Day to the masquerade (193)—took leave &c—

28 T H—Fair & extremely hot for the season—Set off at
six from the New Church Strand—Met several returning
from the masquerade (194)—and a Lady who had been
there came piping hot in the machine to near Newbery
Spinomland (195)—or in Berkshire where we lay—and
near that town I saw turf bog & turf cut thereon—
NB I saw turf also at Reading where we dined—The
Country is very rich from London to this place viz.
Spinomland—yet it is so level that there is scarce a good
prospect the whole way, unless Cleveden (near Maiden-
head bridge) may be so called—Quere is this place the
proud alcove of Shrewsbury & love? (196)

29 T H—Fair but not so warm as yesterday—unless
perhaps the bleakness of Marlborough Downs communicated itself to the air—From near Nubery to near
Cottenham—a space of near 30 miles the country is very
bare of trees & chalkey [?] it is the worst land I have
seen in England, & it is certainly fuller of beggars; for
miles together the coach was pursued by them, from
2 to 9 at a time—almost all of them children—They are
more importunate than in Ireland or even Wales—

30 T H—Heavy rain in the morning—Went to the Abby
church & heared a sorry discourse wretchedly delivered
—Went to the pump room where I met Lady Molyneux
who asked me to dinner—where I spent the pleasantest

day since I came to England for there were five or six
lively Irish girls who sung & danced & did every thing
but ―― Woman are certainly more envious than men,
or at least they discover it upon more trifling occasions—
& they can not bear with patience that one of their party
sh.ᵈ obtain a preference of attention &c—This was
strongly exemplifyed this day—one of these who was a
pretty little coquet—went home after dinner to dress for
the rooms; & her colour was certainly altered on returning for tea—they all fell into a titter & one of them
(who was herself painted as I conceived) cryed out
Heavens look at her cheeks. If she blushed it could not be
seen—But all her varnishing was to no purpose—for she
met not that admiration she expected, & she came back
to supper so cross & peevish that there was no speaking
to her now as after dinner—She sung a song of Cupid
knocking at the door, which was as chaste in the language
as it was bawdy in the Idea; & the *truckle bed* is not more
so; & tho' the girls & even Matrons were kinking with
laughter—she sung on with such a composed gravity as
is the just character of true humour—It is amazing what
pleasure women find in kissing each other; for they do
smack astonishingly

MAY 1.   Fair I believe—tho' I heared there was rain—
I went to Spring gardens in the morning & to the Ball
at the new rooms in the evening—It was very splendid—
for the Duke & Duchess of Cumberland were expected
(but the Duke having sprained his leg at the last did not
come)—but there was the Duke & Duchess of Grafton
& Lady Georgina Fitz-roy, (197) so like the pictures of
Charles the 2d that every body agnized the likeness when

I pointed it out to them—Ld Mahon & his Lady Lord
Chatams daughter (198)—the Beautys were Miss Haywood, the most exquisitely pretty for a fair complexion
I ever saw—She saw me admire & she w^d even come &
sit beside me, yet so innocently sweet was her manner
that it seemed angelic.—Miss Wroughton—that I think
is the name—was rather the brunette beauty but she
discovered such sensibility of mind, & had so much
beauty that I fancy upon acquaintance I sh^d prefer her to
Miss Haywood—Miss Makenzy, neice to Lord Galway,
was a most elegant figure but had not that sweetness of
countenance the two charming English girls possessed—
yet her air & mien was in a grander gusto—Miss Waller
from Ireland was taller—but not to be compared (in my
eye) to any of the three, yet she is preferred by some—
There were four men in the room from one to four inches
taller than myself but whether they were English Irish
or Scotch I know not—NB. Mrs *Hodges*, Miss Luttrell
Lord Thos Clinton &c were there & Mr Garrie greater
than all—to say nothing of Billy Madden who sometime
ago being put in the chair to compromise some dispute
between the room partys; & finding them difficult to be
prevailed on he got up & danced them a hornpipe, which
put them at once into a good temper &c (199)—

MAY 2. Fair & hot—walked out to see Mrs Anderson
—she seems, poor woman, oppressed with affliction—
Dined with Larman where I met a Mr Goddard (200) a
country clergyman very like Dean Langton—who w^d
scarce believe me that I was an Irishman—And in the
evening I walked with him to see the baths, hospital,
minerva's head &c—which he was desirous I sh^d see

Dr Campbell's Diary

before I left Bath—I find it w^d be an easy matter to scrape up acquaintances enow here—for I was asked to dinner for the whole week—so that I was nearly tempted to stay for at least another week

MAY 3. a very light rain about 8 oclock—Came to Bristol & from thence to the Hot Wells—the waters have little of the mineral taste & nothing so warm as those of Bath—by the way Bath itself is not so strong— at least of the sulphur—as Bellnassuttock or Swadlinbar —But Clifton & about the Well is romantically pretty— for England—all of which except about Bath & Bristol are quite level—around Bath are much steeper hills than about Ballynure but the hills & the valleys also are much larger—The steeples of Bristol are elegant modern gothic—The cloysters round the College—i.e. I suppose the collegiate church (now the cathedral) are in part remaining & the College gate is in a grand style— College green is pleasant & the view of Clifton & the environs is very fine, but not in so superlative a degree as I have heared represented

MAY 4. Set off at 4 from Bristol—The morning so foggy that I could not see the country till we came to Newport, the breakfast stage—The Country from thence to Gloucester is a cold wet clay, almost all under grazing, & tho' well planted yet it is a dreary tract, with few houses & those like waste offices—but from Glocester to Tewksbury the looks of the country improve & from Tewksbury to Worcester is by far the most beautiful I have seen in England—it is not like the country round London a dead flat, nor like that round Bath all hill &

90

dale, but there is a wide plain, along the banks of that fine river the Severn, & rising hills interspersed till at length the prospect terminates in mountains of a very varyed outline—so that here we have the 1st 2d & 3d distances, essential to all first rate landskips—Worcester is a pleasant looking town or rather city with 12 or 13 churches beside the meeting houses of nonconformists— here is a great manufactory of gloves & another of carpeting—It seems a thriving town, not like Gloucester, which is evidently declining there being therein but six churches now whereas there were once twelve—but the Cathedral or College as they call it, is magnificently beautiful. The Gothic ornaments are of the airiest sort; but if it be the lightest church without it is the heaviest within I ever saw—the cylindrical pillars in the body of the church are massive beyond all proportion—I can not close this days article without observing that the city of Bristol afforded fewer pretty women than I c^d have expected; nay in truth they all seemed rather ordinary— whereas in Tewkesbury & Worcester the people are in general comely—They nearest answer the descriptions Mr Addison or any other fond Englishman gives of his own country—Here also I observe the greatest (indeed the only) courtesy I have met from the Vermin of Inns— all which however I attribute to the Army which constantly lyes here—& to the officers who (I see) frequent this house. The tone of servitude was here so submissive, so unlike England & so like Ireland, that I was driven to account for it in the manner I have done—Like causes like effects—NB. At Bristol this morning when a passenger made to go into the coach, the Boot-catch took a hold of the mans hand, saying you shant open that door

evening in the parish church I expected the Preacher w^d have begun to spell

8 T H. small rain in the evening at Conway—where the cooking was execrable—Here as in every other part of Wales few of the natives can speak English—The women wear hats like mens, & all the young ones have ruddy Complexions, but not clear—the blood being broke in the cheeks—The Fingallians are most undoubtedly originated from Wales—for they have a family likeness

9 T H Rain in the morning—dined at Widow Knowles' in Gwinda, where every thing was better than I met in any other part of England—and the hostess herself discovered such a goodness of mind that she redeems in my thoughts the character of Publican

[Passage upside down—see page 108]

[Out of place—see page 83]

NB. In October 1776 I went the 2d time to London to publish the *Philosophical Survey* &c—& staid there till May 1777.

[On a separate sheet]

The fact justifies this assertion, [perhaps referring to the discussion on 28 March 1775] for in France they are more annoyed by inclemency of season than in England, & in England than Ireland. It may not be impertinent here to observe, (for the sake of those who are daily complaining of the Irish climate) that in the first week of August 1776 I reaped my oats at Killyvan in the county of Monaghan—that on the first of October following I set out for England, by the road through Scotland—

I loitered with friends to the 7th before I reached
Donaghadee—and in all that road, through great part
of the province of Ulster, I did not see a Stock of any
sort of grain standing in the field. In Scotland the case
was otherwise, much was gathered in to the yards, but
much was also standing in the fields. But what was my
surprise, when I got into England, & not only saw them
in the heat of their oaten harvest, but I also saw in many
places, about *Longtown* particularly & so on to Carlisle,
the stocks of barley or bere standing in the fields. Here
it is to be observed that all this difference c^d not proceed
from climate, in the north of England & the south of
Scotland, it is to be attributed to the genius of the soils—
In that part of Scotland which I noted, the soil was light
& gravelly, in England it was a stiff clay. yet of both
places it is said that the Corn ripens by the Moon
light—

[Regular Diary, out of place]

Again I went there in May 1781 to look for some
preferment for my nephew Tom Campbell (203)—& that
worthy man Mr Alex. Scott of James Street Bedford row
procured him a Cadet's place in the service of the East
India Company—*I staid but a fortnight* or so in London

[On separate sheets] (204)

JUNE 11TH 1781—Went to see Dr Johnson—found
him alone—Barretti came soon after—Barretti (after
some pause in conversation) asked me if the *disturbances*
were over in Ireland—I told him I had not hear'd of any
disturbances there: What! says he, have you not been
up in arms? Yes! and a great number of men continue
so to be. And dont you call that disturbance, returned

Dr Campbell's Diary

Barretti? No! said I. The Irish Volunteers have de-
meaned themselves very peacibly, & instead of dis-
turbing the peace of the country have contributed much
to its preservation. The Doctor who had been long
silent, turned a sharp ear to what I was saying, & with
vehemence said—What Sir dont you call it disturbance
to oppose legal government with arms in your hands,
& compel it to make laws in your favour? Sir *I* call it
Rebellion—Rebellion as much as the rebellions of Scotland. Doctor, said I, I am sorry to hear that fall from
you; I must, however, say that the Irish consider themselves as the most loyal of his Majesties subjects, at the
same time that they firmly deny any allegiance to a
British parliament. They have a separate legislature &
that they have never shewed any inclination to resist—
Sir, says the Doctor, you *do owe allegiance* to the *British*
parliament, as a *conquered* nation; (205) & had I been
minister I would have made you submit to it, I would
have done as Oliver Cromwell did, I would have burned
your cities, & roasted you in the fires or flames of
them. (206)—I, after allowing the Doctor to vent his
indignation upon Ireland, coolly replyed—Doctor the
times are altered, & I dont find that you have succeeded
so well in burning the cities & roasting the inhabitants
of America.—Sir, (says he, gravely & with a less vehement tone) what you say is true, the times are altered,
for *Power* is now nowhere. We live under a government
of *influence* not of power. (207) But, Sir, had we treated
the Americans as we ought & as they deserved we sh^d
have at once razed all their towns &c &c—& let them
enjoy their forests &c—after this wild rant, argument
w^d but have enraged him, I therefore let him vibrate into

stay there I set out with Sr Capel Molyneux to the North in his way to Ireland, intending to return to London to be more explicit with the Booksellers, or one of them, as to the immediate publication of a first Volume, which I thought was ready—but having some conversations with Mr Thorkelin, the Icelander, (209) relative to some disputed points of the most remote Antiquity, relative to which he promised to procure me Certain documents from Denmark; & ruminating on the propriety or impropriety of publishing one volume alone, which w^d have reached only to Henry 7th, I no sooner found myself in Edenburgh than I resolved to return home with the worthy Baronet—though I had left all my papers in London—so that my progress was interrupted—

[An expense account kept on separate small sheets]

1786 Novr the 13th viz monday set out from the Devizes—Where I rec^d from Sr Capel Molyneux five guineas towards payment of the bills for expences on the road &c &c—

NB. P^d for the receipt	2–8½	Monday at Devizes *	£0–11–9
		D^o at Malmsbury—	2–10
		Tuesday Glocester—	13–7
NB. Snow &c—		D^o Upton—	2–4
* Sr C. a guinea!		Wednesday Birmingham—	14–9
at the Peacock 10^s 0		Thursday Litchfield	13–3
		D^o the 16th Derby—	2–2
Stockings 8^d—		Friday Peacock—	11–3
		D^o Sheffield—	2–0
		Saturday Barnsley—	8–7½
		D^o Wakefield—	2–6

£4–5–0½

Dr Campbell's Diary

Nov.ʳ 19th, *Sunday*,

Harrogate—	12–0
Dᵒ Ripon—	2–0
Monday 20th Darlington *	9–6
Dᵒ Durham—	2–6
Tuesday Newcastle—	17–0
Wednesday Morpeth—	9–0
Dᵒ Alnewich—	4–6
Thursday Berwick—	14–5
Friday the 24 Haddington	11–6

* NB. There we met Lady Strathmore &c—

4–2–5

NB. Sir Capel gave there to the Stock purse four guineas—

Edinburgh Nov.ʳ 27–86

Dunn's Hotel—	£3–13–2
NB. a Cadet—	–6
Dᵒ Levingston—	2–0
Glasgow—	10–6
Dᵒ at the high Kirk—	1–0
Wednesday 29 Ayr—	10–0
Thursday Girvan—	9–8
Dᵒ Balantray—	2–0
Stranrawer—Dec. 1st	11–0

5–19–8

First subscription	£10–10–0
Second Dᵒ	6–6–0
	16–16–0

From which deducting the Bills as ℞ contra 15–11–5½

Port Patrick—	14–0
Donaghadee—	3–0

NB. forgot the sum given to servants at Edinburgh 7–4

1–4–4

Remains of whole contribution	1–4–6½

Brought over—	5–19–8
Dᵒ—	4–2–5
Dᵒ—	4–5–0½

The half of which is due to Sʳ Capel 12–3¼

Total of the Bills £15–11–5½

public buildings—particularly the *Hal de Ble*—are magnificent—The chappel of the Virgin in the Church of St Sulpice far above the force of my imagination—no wonder that the Devotees there kissed the ground at their departure from—it was heaven upon earth in miniature—the Dome of the Invalids fine & grand but in the former respect not to be compared to this inimitable *Morcieu* NB. The *Hal de Ble* is 40 yards or 120 feet under the cupola, besides the concentrical exterior area in colonnade—this sh^d have been the model for our *Rotunda*—St Eustace comes next to St Sulpice—the view of the East window, through the high Altar is solemn as to impress devotion—NB. on a view of St Sulpice the ceiling appeared to me too low, & as it wanted the gothic ramifications to give it lightness it might have appeared heavy to me even if had been high enough—but the chappel of St Mary the more I saw it the more I liked it —it is the most happy combination of Architecture sculpture & painting—*decies repetita placebit* (212)—it never lost its enchantment—it enwrapped me each time more & more, & made me almost pardon the idolatries of popery—The Notre Dame is a magnificent pile NB. from the Steeple Paris does not appear to me half as large i.e. not to cover half the ground as London does from St Pauls—but then the houses in Paris are twice as high as those in London & the streets appear more populous—The Dome & Church in the Sorbonne, built by Cardinal Richlieu is well worth seeing—not only for the Cardinals monument of parian marble in the center of the Choir with his Statue in a recumbent posture (his beautiful neice in the character of) Religion supporting his head & Science weeping at his feet, with her book

cast aside &c—but for the statues of the 4 evangelists &
12 apostles—the pictures but midling

ON SUNDAY THE 22D OF JULY 87 I went to the
Anniversary celebration of St James's day at his church
of the Bucheries—high Mass is mere Mummery—the
Musick was said to be fine, but I dont understand musick
—The Mode of collecting the alms alone struck me &
was indeed a reflected image of the Despotism, the
Superstition & the gallantry of the nation—The Swiss
Halberdier struck the ground every now & then with his
halbert to make way for a Clerical-like person who led
in his hand a beautiful little girl who carried a scrip or
bag to receive the alms—The Swiss commanded awe,
the Gownsman reminded you to contribute & the pretty
female by her looks told you sure you cant refuse—

ON TUESDAY THE 24TH I went to the Parliament
house with Mͬ Blakeway (213) & after waiting four hours
& more saw what—why Monsieur, Count D Artois
Bishop of Paris &c come out after their deliberations on
the Remonstrance against the Stamp duty &c—

WEDNESDAY THE 25TH went to Versailes with
Mͬ Smyth (214)—was much disappointed at the sight of
the palace—the outside is great, but not magnificent &
the inside tawdry not beautiful—The gardens in the old
square style, thickly studded with statues,—the only
thing in true taste was the grotto of Louis 14 where he
is represented in the character of Apollo coming out of
the bath attended by six Nymphs with his horses in two
caves on each sᵈ that large one, wherein was the Groupe
of the vain Monarch in the character of a God—& under

whose statue in the Place de Victoire is the inscription
Viro immortali—

[A separate sheet]

ON MONDAY JULY THE 30TH 1787 between eleven
& twelve o'clock I left Paris—at eight next day I got to
Roan, where I spent two hours, viewing the Cathedral,
Tombs &c—& during that interval became acquainted
with M.ʳ Sturgeon husband to Lady Harriot Wentworth (215)—He shewed me much affection as a country-
man & especially as he knew my brother.—He told me
that specimens of English Cotton fabricks had been inter-
mixed with French, & submitted to the inspection of
certain officers in Roan, whose business it is to estimate
their value & fix their price—& that these officers not
suspecting them to be English rated them at 20 £ ℔ cwt
above the French—When this took wind it gave a
dreadful alarm to the Normans.

ON WEDNESDAY THE 1ST OF AUGUST about one
oClock I found myself at Brighthelmston—so that in a
little more than 48 hours I passed from Paris to [torn
sheet]—That night (viz Wednesday) I went to the Ball
with S.ʳ Boyle Roach—where there was but a small party,
but these mostly of the prime of Britain & France—viz.,
the Prince of Wales, Duke & Duchess of Cumberland—
the Princess of Lambal who (it is said) was married
(& but for a few months) to the son of the Duke of
Ponthievre, whose daughter is married to the Duke of
Orleans—in her suite were three French Ladies of quality
—Besides these recited, were the Duke of Bedford, Duke
of Queensbury & other Nobles, particularly Lords *Maynard* & Clermont—Lest it sh.ᵈ be forgotten I set it down

that when I came into the room Mrs Fitzherbert sat in
the highest seat at the top of the room with the Duke of
Cumberland—The Prince was standing in the circle of
ladys &c—[torn sheet] the Duchess of Rutland was by
far the fairest of the fair—Mrs Fitzherbert did not dance
the first set—but the second she danced with Isaac Corry,
& after dancing down, she sat down with her partner,
& in a few minutes the Prince & the Duke of Cumberland
came & sat beside her—The Prince expressed affection
in his looks, & the Duke esteem—She discovers strong
sensibility & considerable dignity in her countenance &
deportment—NB. The general appearance of the English
was to my eye, fresh from Paris, what it never before
had been, strangely awkward & clownish, at this ball—
The French deserve most richly that character of pre-
eminent politeness which they have universally obtained
—I never saw a awkward person in France even in the
lowest department—They are, upon the whole, a strange
but agreeable mixture of pomp & beggary—the latter is
visible in every avenue of Versailles, even in the Palace—
I listened in the street to a woman who sung ballads,
with the assistance of her husbands tambour, with more
pleasure than I ever did at Ranelagh, Vauxhall or the
Rotunda—The French language & Musick seem adapted
to engage the heart in small matters &c—

But to return to Brighton—It was irritating my feelings
to see C. Fox walking on the Steyne on Thursday night
with a vulgar looking *Putain*, a whore more mean
looking than one of 2–6 on the strand, with Lord
Clermont (216) & the first of nobility, (viz. the Duke of
Bedford) sneaking along with this profligate head of

opposition—no wonder that the Duke of Bedford sh^d glory in a like practice, & that Ld Maynard (217) sh^d not only glory in his gilded horn, but that he sh^d serve as Pimp to this Duke of fifty thousand a year—

[Regular Diary again]

NB. The churches of Amiens & Rouen, especially the former sh^d detain the traveller—

ON MONDAY JULY THE 30TH between 11 & 12 I left Paris & on Wednesday the first of Augt about one oclock I found myself at Brighthelmstone, so that after spending two hours at Rouen & more at Dieppe I passed from Paris to Brighton in about 49 hours—This is scarce worthy notice—but upon the whole I must observe that according to the impressions made upon me in this short excursion the two countries bear an exact image of the governments in each—In England the laws are made by the people & therefore they are there for the people & their interests—In France the people are only considered as if made for the use of the court of Versailles & city of Paris—& therefore the people of France do not reflect that image of happiness which the English nation does in every quarter—& yet it is said that the English are less happy than the French—now, though I dont believe this, yet it possibly may be the case—for the English are so pampered by a redundance of meat & money, that they may be said at all times to be under a plethora of both, & therefore may not enjoy that happiness which is within their reach—The laws too being made by & for them (as I have observed) gives them frequent advantages, on trials by jury, over their superiors in rank, which renders them rough & savage in their manners &

like children *wilful* peevish & discontented, repining at
their own inferiority of condition, & of course unhappy in
their stations; not considering that an equality of ranks is
incompatible with any form of society ever yet established—Which verifies the French Maxim "Tout chose
a le bon & le mal."—

I have thought that if the persons & things of both
countries be supposed to be divided into ten classes,
there will be found in France one class of these to be so
superior to any thing of the kind in England as to have
no parallel there—another class may be found in both
countries perfectly on *par*,—but that the remaining eight
classes in the lower walks of life will be found every way
superior in England—That is to say, among the mass
of the people, which I count as *eight*, the whole advantage
as to the means of the comforts & conveniencies of life
lie on the side of the English—And to explain myself as
to that highest rank in France for which, I say, England
can produce no parallel, I instance in the pomp of a court,
the elegance of mind & manners prevalent among the
highest orders in France, the general refinement among
the more numerous orders of clergy & lawyers, the
unrivaled accomplishments of the female sex which more
than compensates for that beauty of person which dis-
tinguishes English ladies, but which is rarely embellished
by that expressive eye & those acquired accomplishments
which characterize the French Ladies & place th^m not
only above competition in the present age, but challenge
antiquity to produce any thing equal to them—NB.
I speak of classes of persons & things not of individuals—
England may & I doubt not does produce individuals

equal to any in any other country—but elegance (I dont mean cleanliness, on which the English pride themselves) of ranks is not as yet to be found in England—The Gentry are cold, lifeless & reserved—the *mauvais honte* is still prevalent among them—They may perhaps in general see what is decorous in behaviour, but they have not acquired the habits of it—of this they are conscious, & therefore they are generally stiff, if not awkward, in their carriage; & always afraid of being incorrect they seldom arrive at excellence, in the exhibition of those good qualities, which they frequently possess.—The French most richly deserve that character of superlative politeness which they have obtained—the dispotism of their government has contributed to it—they are compelled to restrain those ebulitions of passion, which sometimes disfigure the behaviour of a free people & this general awe, with which they are impressed, smooths the perturbations of the mind & disposes the people to suavity of demeanour & to those resources from the anguish of thought upon public affairs which is only to be found in the mutual endearments of private society—

My Sixth visit to England was in the end of the year 1789 with Dᴿ Hales & his Sisters—spent my Christmas in Bath—went up to London the night before the Queens Birthday when I had my pockets picked of 12½ guineas— my Sardonix ring—& the Medal of the king of Morocco which Col. Vallancy called the Talisman—

My seventh Visit to England was in consequence of a wish expressed by the Bishop of Dromore (218) that I should meet him there & bring with the Life of Dᴿ Gold-

Dr Campbell's Diary

smith, which I had compiled from documents furnished by him that it might be published with his works by Nichols, for the benefit of his brothers (particularly Maurice who had been in the habit of getting subscriptions before I undertook the task) & sisters—on the 20th Febry 1792 I sailed with Mrs Kerr, & remarkable it is that on the 27th, the same day on which the Parliament house in Dublin was burned, We arrived at the Bear in Bath—on the 19th of March we set out for London, where we staid only to the 25th—& on Saturday morning the 31 arrived in Dublin—where, on the next day I heard Mr. Kirwan (219) preach, in his turn as Chaplain, before the Ld Lieutenant (220) in the Castle chappel—The subject of his discourse was the influence of the manners of high stations upon the low—The Preacher pointed almost personally to the Chief Governor & even mimickd his awkward attitudes & ridiculd his mode of spending his time—After his first *rest* he recepitulated what he had said on the baleful example of high stations in the country—& then turning to the gallery where his excellency sat, he said—I ask you what examples do you set to this country—& after a long pause, he repeated I ask you what examples do you in high station set to the people of this country

[Misc. observations]

To upbraid people for want of antientry of blood is like chiding the Thames because his stream is beggarly at Reading—a thought—People are some times rather passive than active in the operation of their Genius— The human frame is a machine which set in motion runs on without any spontaneity—Hence all those flashes

107

NOTES

A NOTE ON THE DOCUMENTATION

NO ATTEMPT has been made to provide a note, with the full name and identification, for every person mentioned in the Diary. For well-known people, members of the nobility, etc., the first names and titles will merely be included in the index. Where identification has been difficult, or is uncertain, a note will explain the problem.

The following abbreviations have been used:

Life: J. Boswell, *The Life of Samuel Johnson, LL.D.*, ed. G.B. Hill, revised and enlarged by L. F. Powell (Oxford, 1934).

Private Papers: Private Papers of James Boswell from Malahide Castle, ed. Geoffrey Scott and Frederick A. Pottle (privately printed, 1928–34).

Letters: Letters of Samuel Johnson, LL.D., ed. G.B. Hill (Oxford, 1892).

John. Misc: Johnsonian Miscellanies, ed. G.B. Hill (Oxford, 1897).

Kent: An Encyclopaedia of London, ed. William Kent (London, 1937).

Illustrations: J. Nichols, *Illustrations of the Literary History of the Eighteenth Century* (London, 1817–58).

Thraliana: Thraliana, The Diary of Mrs Hester Lynch Thrale (Later Mrs. Piozzi), ed. K. C. Balderston (Oxford, 1942).

1 Hippocras, an old cordial made of spiced wine with other ingredients, sometimes used as an emetic.

2 Henry Flood (1732–91), Irish statesman and orator, quarrelled bitterly with James Agar over an election contest. A duel was fought, in which Agar was slightly wounded; then in 1769 a second duel was arranged and Agar was killed. According

Notes on the Diary

to contemporary accounts Agar was a violent man and his language most insulting and unwarrantable, so that Flood was not to blame in the affair. He was, however, tried for murder at the Assizes of Kilkenny, where the jury found him guilty of manslaughter in his own defence—a virtual acquittal. For a sketch of his political life see *Gent. Mag.* LXI (Dec. 1791), 1224–33. See also Charles Phillips, *Curran and His Contemporaries*.

3   For Johnson's and Mrs Thrale's impressions of North Wales see A. M. Broadley, *Dr Johnson and Mrs Thrale*, 1910.

4   The tree had been cut down in 1756 by Francis Gastrel. The wood was afterwards purchased by Thomas Sharp who made a considerable sum by converting it into small boxes. See *Life*, II, 541. Also E. Law, *Shakespeare's Garden*, 1922, pp. 8–10.

5   'Good Friend, for Jesus' sake forbear
             To dig the dust enclosed here:
             Blest be the man that spares these stones,
             And curst be he that moves my bones.'

For a description of the church and the monuments in it, see E. I. Fripp, *Shakespeare's Stratford*, 1928, pp. 66–75.

6   The bust was the work of Gerard Johnson, son of a Dutch tomb-maker in Southwark, near the Globe Theatre. Fripp suggests that the King's Men may have had a hand in the monument. The inscription is as follows:

'Judicio Pylium, genio Socratem, arte Maronem,
   Terra tegit, populus maeret, Olympus habet.

Stay Passenger, why goest thou by so fast?
Read if thou canst whom envious Death hath plac'd
Within this monument: Shakespeare! with whom
Quick Nature died, whose name doth deck this tomb
Far more than cost; sith all that he hath writ
Leaves living Art but page to serve his Wit....'

(Fripp, *op. cit.* pp. 74–5.)

7   'Ten-in-the-Hundred must lie in his grave,
     But a hundred to ten, whether God will him have.
     Who then must be interr'd within this tomb?
     "Oh, oh," quoth the Devil, "my John a Combe!"'

This doggerel was fastened on his tomb sometime before 1618, and was ascribed to Shakespeare before the year 1634. See Fripp, *op. cit.* p. 64.

Notes on the Diary

8 Possibly this was Henry Barnard, son of the Bishop of Derry, though we have no evidence that he was in Oxford at the time. He was a student at Trinity College at the same time as Campbell.

9 Conway's seat was called 'Park Place'. John Wesley wrote in his Journal for 19 Oct. 1784: 'I spent an hour at Lord Harcourt's seat, near Nuneham, one of the pleasantest spots I have seen. It stands on a gently rising hill and commands a most delightful prospect.'

10 The *Public Advertiser* for Thursday, 2 March, announced that at the Theatre Royal in Covent Garden that day would be performed a new tragedy called *Cleonice* (by John Hoole). Mrs Barry was in the cast. But since Campbell makes no comment on the play, it is doubtful if he attended the performance.

11 On the 11th Campbell calls him 'my old College friend'. He would thus be John Day, who entered Trinity College, Dublin, 11 Dec. 1752, and received his B.A. in the spring of 1757 (*Alumni Dublinenses*).

12 Hugh Kelly, dramatist, rival of Goldsmith, who died in 1777.

13 The old Hummums, in the eastern corner of Covent Garden, had been destroyed by fire in March 1769. 'Mr Rigg's Hummum', however, had been shortly after rebuilt as an hotel. See A. Dobson, 'The Tour of Covent Garden', *Eighteenth Century Vignettes*, 3rd series, pp. 332–4.

14 For an account of The Grecian Coffee House see W. Kent, *An Encyclopaedia of London*, 1937, pp. 627–8. It was so called from a Greek named Constantine who kept it in the seventeenth century. It became noted as a place where literary men forgathered, and is mentioned by Addison and Steele, Goldsmith, etc. See also Boswell, *Private Papers*, x, 188; xvii, 104; xviii, 81.

15 *Braganza*, by Robert Jephson, an Irishman, is described by D. E. Baker, *Biographia Dramatica*, 1812, ii, 66, as very successful in 1775, but falling soon into neglect. The plot was too much like that of *Venice Preserved*. The *Morning Post* of 4 March advertises the tenth night of the tragedy, to which is also added the thirteenth performance of a new comic opera called *The Rival Candidates*, by Henry Bate, with music by Thomas Carter.

16 Full accounts of the affair appeared in the newspapers. The *Morning Chronicle* for Monday, 6 March states: 'DRURY LANE—

111

Notes on the Diary

The performance of the entertainment at this theatre did not end on Saturday evening till eleven o'clock. The audience was detained till that late hour on account of Mrs. Yates's having left the theatre as soon as she had finished her part, without speaking the Epilogue. The house was clamorous and would not give up their right. Mr. Vernon endeavoured to appease their fury, by declaring that "Mrs. Yates being taken with a hoarseness, had left the theatre." This excuse had been so frequently made on similar occasions, and had so frequently been afterwards discovered to be a mere stage trick, that the audience would not accept it, but still insisted on Mrs. Yates's coming on to do her duty. Mr. Vernon then withdrew, and, after a short time, returned, assuring the house that he had sent to Mr. Garrick, (who was confined to his room with a fit of the Scone [*sic*], but) who had directed the messenger immediately to fetch Mrs. Yates, and that her husband was then in the theatre. He was directly called for, and instantly came on the stage to know the pleasure of the audience. They told him bluntly, "they did not want to see him, but to hear his wife, whose obstinacy and pride had betrayed her into the present insult." He in vain endeavoured to assure them, that both Mrs. Yates and himself wish'd only to know the will of the Town, to obey it; that her conduct on the present occasion proceeded from a very contrary cause to that which they alledged, that the cause was real illness, and that she was in bed when he left her. They then said "bring her and the bed together." As the clamour was universal, Mr. Yates quitted the stage; and after the orchestra had once or twice in vain endeavoured to play the Overture to the Rival Candidates, Weston walked on and began to speechify. He was treated like a field preacher—most plentifully pelted. With great coolness he picked up the missile weapons (which consisted chiefly of apples and oranges) and, after filling his pockets with them, walked off roaring out, "'Tis cruel to hurt us for Mrs. Yates; she'll be here on Monday to answer for herself." At length, an hour and a half having been spent in tumult, the overture was suffered, and the Farce went on, but not in silence.' See also *London Chronicle*, 4–7 March, *Gazetteer*, 6 March, and *Morning Post*, 6 March. These all publish letters from Mrs Yates protesting her illness.

Such disturbances seem not to have been unusual, for the *Morning Chronicle* for 8 March reported that 'Monday night a mischievous person threw an apple from the front of the upper gallery at Covent Garden theatre, which struck a violin, worth upwards of ten guineas, while one of the performers was playing on it, and broke it to pieces.'

17   Possibly Matthew Pearson of Dublin (B.A. Trinity College 1742, admitted to the Irish Bar, 1747), though it is impossible to identify him more completely.

18   Thomas Thurlow, afterwards Bishop of Durham.

19   In the voyage to Brobdingnag, the dwarf had wedged Gulliver into an empty marrow bone.

20   Possibly Gamble, who is mentioned again on the 10th. A Robert Gamble of Dublin was in college with Campbell (*Alumni Dublinenses*).

21   Francis Andrews, M.P. for Derry, and Provost of Trinity College, was a lawyer of wit and accomplishments, who exercised considerable influence at Dublin during Lord Townshend's administration. (F. Hardy, *Memoirs of Lord Charlemont*, 2nd ed. I, 147.)

22   For further accounts of Rigby, etc. see Hardy, *op. cit.* I, 104 ff.

23   John Russell, 4th Duke of Bedford. For his aid to Rigby, etc. see *D.N.B.*

24   The play was *Zara*, a tragedy by Aaron Hill, taken from Voltaire's *Zaire*. Garrick played Lusignan and Miss Younge, Zara. The doors of the theatre were advertised in the newspapers as opening at five o'clock with the performance beginning at six. Evidently Campbell was not able to get a seat, since he first saw Garrick on the 14th.

25   *Morning Chronicle*, 8 March: 'Yesterday their Majesties took an airing in a coach to Kew and Richmond, and returned to the Queen's Palace to dinner.'
In his succeeding references to King George III, Campbell is always respectful, and makes no mention of His Majesty's mental troubles. Some of the newspapers of the day were far less discreet. See also the *Morning Post* for 5 April 1775.

26   Dolly's Chop-House is mentioned three times in Boswell's *Private Papers* and seems to have been a popular eating place in London. Musgrave, in listing the death of the proprietress, speaks of her as 'Dolly, the Chop House woman'.

Notes on the Diary

27   The *Daily Advertiser*, 8 March: 'To be Sold by Auction by Mess. Langford at their House in the Great Piazza, Covent Garden, this and the following Evenings, by Order of the Executors, The Collection of Prints, Drawings, and Books of Prints of the Rev. Henry Burroughs, D.D. late of Wisbech, in the Isle of Ely. To be viewed till the Sale, which will begin at Six o'Clock.'

28   The initials are almost impossible to decipher. Raymond read T— B—, but S—t seems more likely. Possibly it was Alexander Scott. See n. 40.

29   John Stanley. See n. 32.

30   Advertised in the *Morning Chronicle* for 16 March: 'Amongst the great additions to the MUSEUM in Spring Garden, which is now in the utmost state of accumulated slendour, is the superb Horse and Tent.'

31   *Daily Advertiser*, 10 March: 'Christie's rooms—a valuable collection of paintings of Thomas Bladen Esq., also some of a nobleman containing pictures of Rembrandt, Cuyp, Poussin, Guercino, Caracci, Guido &c.'

32   Under 'Oratorio Intelligence' the *Morning Post* of 4 March had stated: 'Mr. Stanley opened his Oratorio campaign last night at the Theatre Royal Drury-lane, with the admired sacred Drama of *Judas Machaboeus*: his principal performers were Mrs. Mattocks, Mrs. Barthelemon, a Young Lady, Mr. Reinhold, and Mr. Norris. We cannot so well relish the present vocal substitutes, when we consider the admirable performances of this divine composition two seasons past, and the appearance of the house last night seems to forebode a very different kind of harvest from that which was then reaped. Indeed the chaste attention of the band, Mr. Stanley's organ, and Mr. Barthelemon's violin concertos, together with the pleasing hautboy solo by Mr. Vincent, a man of uncommon diffidence in his profession, are the principal, if not the only inducement that can draw a man this season to Mr. Stanley's Oratorios at Drury-lane.'

The performance on 10 March was advertised in the *Gazetteer* as 'By Command of Their Majesties'. It began at 6.30. See also *Morning Chronicle*, 31 March.

33   The British Coffee House, in Cockspur Street, was largely frequented by Scotsmen. It is mentioned by Boswell in his *Private Papers*, XIV, 172, 183–4. See also *N. & Q.* for 17 July 1920.

Notes on the Diary

34 There was no one named Mayne representing Scotland in Parliament at this time. The man referred to was probably Robert Mayne who served for Gatton in Surrey, in place of his brother Sir William Mayne, who served for Canterbury. They were both natives of Scotland, having been born in county Clackmannan. In a speech on American affairs Sir William once spoke of his having been born on the other side of the Tweed. (Raymond, p. 121.)

35 James Macpherson's *History of Great Britain from the Restoration to the Accession of the House of Hannover*, published by Strahan and Cadell, is listed in the newspapers as having been published 10 March 1775. See *Gazetteer* and *Morning Chronicle*. It was issued in two large volumes, quarto, price two guineas.

36 At this time the Scotch were violent in denunciations of Johnson because of his recently published *Journey to the Western Islands of Scotland*, in which he attacked the authenticity of Ossian and was in general not very complimentary about the country. The London newspapers had been full of bitter rejoinders from Scotch correspondents. As samples, the *Morning Chronicle* for 25 January contained an angry assault on Johnson for his incredulity about Macpherson; and the next day referred to 'this malevolent, hellish turn of mind'. The *Morning Post* for 27 January guessed that if Lord Bute had known of what Johnson was to write, the pension would never have been given.

37 It had been published on 8 March (*Life*, II, 515).

38 I can find no reference in the newspapers to this particular incident, but the *Gazetteer* on 3 February had commented: 'An altercation ensued between Mr. Burke and Sir William Bagot, as to a Mr. T——r who had signed the Birmingham petition; they both were very warm in support of their arguments, but were called to order by the Speaker.' The quotation was a combination of the *Book of Common Prayer* versions of Psalms 39.2 and 116.10.

39 For information about the Foundling Hospital see J.H. Hutchins, *Jonas Hanway*, 1940, pp. 16–46.

40 Alexander Scott of James Street, Bedford Row, had been elected a Governor of the Foundling Hospital in 1767. (R.H. Nichols and F.A. Wray, *History of the Foundling Hospital*, 1935, p. 380.)

41 A German traveller, Sophie v. la Roche, in 1786 was much struck by the lighting and paving of Oxford Street. As translated,

Notes on the Diary

her comments were: 'We strolled up and down lovely Oxford Street this evening, for some goods look more attractive by artificial light. Just imagine, dear children, a street taking half an hour to cover from end to end, with double rows of brightly shining lamps, in the middle of which stands an equally long row of beautifully lacquered coaches, and on either side of these there is room for two coaches to pass one another; and the pavement, inlaid with flagstones, can stand six people deep and allows one to gaze at the spledidly lit shop fronts in comfort.' (Kent, p. 336.)

42   Possibly Richard Combe, who in 1780 became treasurer and paymaster of his Majesty's Office of Ordnance. See *Gent. Mag.* L (Sept. 1780), 447. See also page 63 of *Diary*.

43   Blackfriars Road had only recently been formed, in pursuance of an Act of 1769. It led from St George's Fields northward to Blackfriars Bridge, which itself had been completed in 1770. (Kent, pp. 64, 589.)

44   *Gent. Mag.* XLVIII (Sept. 1778), 440, lists under Bankrupts 'Joseph Jacob and John Viny, Black-Friars-bridge, wheel-manufacturers.'

45   See n. 77.

46   Modern scholars would scarcely call Mrs Thrale 'learned', although she could read some Latin and had a wide, if not very thorough, knowledge of literature. Yet she certainly gave the impression of being highly educated to strangers. Thus a German traveller, Helferich Peter Sturz, in 1768 wrote of meeting Johnson: 'auf dem Landgute des Herrn Thrailes, dessen Frau griechisch zum Zeitvertreib liest.' (H. P. Sturz, *Kleine Schriften*, Leipzig, 1904, p. 97.)

47   James Northcote, in his *Life of Sir Joshua Reynolds*, 1818, I, 317, records that Thrale once gave a dinner at the brewery, at which the guests, who included Reynolds, Johnson, Goldsmith, Garrick, Burke, Baretti, 'dined on beef-steaks broiled on the coppers, seated in a newly made brewing vessel, sufficiently capacious to contain the company conveniently'.

48   Possibly Hugh Boyd (see *D.N.B.*) who had been educated at Trinity College, Dublin. Some people attributed the *Letters of Junius* to him.

Notes on the Diary

49   The play was John Fletcher's *Rule a Wife and Have a Wife* (*Morning Post*, 14 March 1775). Raymond in 1854 misread the manuscript of the Diary, and printed the part played by Garrick as Lear instead of Leon. As a result, critics ever since have been puzzled as to why Campbell thought Lear was not a part in which the actor could display himself. The play was followed by the two-act Opera, *The Rival Candidates*, with Dodd in the cast. See *Drury Lane Calendar*, ed. D. MacMillan, 1938, pp. 316, 320.

50   Charles Congreve, who later became Chaplain to Archbishop Boulter and Archdeacon of Armagh, was a year or so older than Johnson and left Lichfield School for Oxford in March 1725/26. For a full account of him see A. L. Reade, *Johnsonian Gleanings*, III, 126–7.

51   James Sims, M.D. (1741–1820). Boswell on 21 August 1790 refers to 'Dr. Simms, the irish City Physician'. (*Private Papers*, XVIII, 90, 94.)

52   John Collins (*D.N.B.*). *The Gazetteer*, Wednesday, 15 March 1775, has the advertisement: 'The Fourth Night. This Evening in the Great Room, at the Devil Tavern, Temple-Bar, will be delivered a Satyrical, critical, mimical, and analytical lecture on the elements of MODERN ORATORY...by the Author, J. Collins. The doors to be opened at half after six o'clock, and the lecture to begin exactly at seven. Admittance half a crown. Tickets to be had at the Devil Tavern.'

The *Morning Chronicle*, for 16 March, contains the remarks: 'A correspondent who was last night at the Devil Tavern lecture remarks, that both Dr. Kenrick and Mr. Collins afford room for laughter, but in a very different manner. The learned Doctor moved the risibility of his auditors by his own ingenious absurdity. Mr. Collins who pretends to nothing more than a happy adoption of old stories, excites laughter by the humorous manner of his in reducing and applying the wit of others. The one lecturer was foiled by being too wise in his own conceit; the other gains real applause by modestly aiming no higher than he can reach.'

For a history of the Devil Tavern see Kent, p. 634.

53   Concerning the offer from Trinity College, in November 1774, see L. Collison-Morley, *Giuseppe Baretti*, 1909, pp. 275–7. Baretti had returned to Italy in 1760 (*Life*, I, 361).

54   G. B. Hill was certain that Chesterfield was referring to George Lyttelton rather than Johnson (*Life*, I, 267). The latest

biographer of Lyttelton, Rose Mary Davis, is undecided, though at least we may be sure the Hottentot was not meant to be Johnson. (*The Good Lord Lyttelton*, Bethlehem, Pa. 1939, pp. 16–18.)

55   See *Life*, III, 357.

56   The London newspapers had been filled with attacks. A writer in the *Morning Chronicle* for 8 March referred to 'Dr. Johnson's pedantic, pompous, and absurd detail of what he *did not see* in Scotland,' and added that the public would not be 'gulled by the *stubborn audacity* of a vain, self created oracle.' Other onslaughts appeared in the *Morning Chronicle* for 11 March; the *Public Advertiser* for 13 March; and *Lloyd's Evening Post* for 13–15 March. The *Morning Post* for 16 March had remarked: 'Dr. Johnson, we hear, intends employing his time the ensuing summer in Ireland; therefore we may naturally hope to be entertained with descriptions of places, &c. in that kingdom, as interesting as those he lately gave us of Scotland.' Johnson had been widely charged with having abused the hospitality of the Scots (*Life*, II, 305–6). There is no evidence that he ever seriously considered a tour of Ireland (*Life*, II, 307; III, 410).

57   Johnson on another occasion spoke slightingly of Dr James Foster, the Nonconformist preacher (*Life*, IV, 9). As Raymond puts it, Campbell, 'although he does not dispute Johnson's estimate of the man, thinks it not meet to have it so set down. The fear of Roman Catholicism has always drawn the bond of union between the Established Church and the Dissenters much closer in Ireland than in England' (p. 34).

58   Many people appear to have suspected Burke. For instance, *Lloyd's Evening Post* for 14–17 April 1775 remarked that Burke was 'thought by some to be the Writer of those Epistles which appeared some years since with the signature of Junius'. For Johnson's subsequent opinion see *Life*, III, 376–7.

59   Richard Burke. For a complete account of him see D. Wecter, *Edmund Burke and His Kinsmen*, 1939, pp. 49–75.

60   In the *Morning Chronicle* for 8 April 1775 appeared the anecdote: 'Some friends mentioning to Dr. Johnson the severe attacks made at his character for his two last publications, he replied, "Let the little dogs bark—I shall eat my dinner."'

61   Frances Reynolds. Burke's speech on American taxation had been made 19 April 1774. His more famous one recommending

Notes on the Diary

conciliation was to be given about a week after this conversation, on 22 March 1775.

62   See Johnson's *Letters*, I, 304–5, 315, 378–9. On 22 December 1774 Johnson had written to Dr Taylor of his meeting with Congreve: 'How long he has been here I know not. . . . He told me he knew not how to find me. . . . He talked to me of theological points, and is going to print a sermon, but I thought he appeared neither very acute nor very knowing. . . .'

63   *Edward and Eleonora*, by James Thomson, had been prohibited by the Lord Chamberlain in 1739. In an altered version by Thomas Hall it was played at Covent Garden for the first time on 18 March 1775, as a benefit for Mrs Barry. See the *Morning Post* for 17 and 18 March. It was followed by the comic opera, *The Padlock*, by Bickerstaffe and Dibden. The *Morning Chronicle* for 20 March stated that *Edward and Eleonora* had been 'received with that best test of excellence, where the tender passions are attempted to be excited,—gushing tears. The audience, which was more brilliant and numerous than any ever yet seen in this theatre, confessed their sensibility, and wept applause.' Mrs Barry was called the 'first actress now living'.

64   See p. 58. The play originally announced was *Zenobia*, but *Timanthes* actually was given.

65   Elizabeth Carter, celebrated for her scholarship, her puddings, and her headaches. See A. C. C. Gaussen, *A Woman of Wit and Wisdom*, 1906.

66   Rev. William Parker (1714–1802), a good friend of Mrs Thrale. In *Thraliana* (p. 20), she wrote: 'Doctor Parker has some pleasant Stories, but he tells them so tediously they give more Disgust than Pleasure.' For a long account of him see *Thraliana*, p. 263.

67   The Rev. Richard Harrison is described in Nichols's *Anecdotes*, IX, 226–7. See also Boswell, *Private Papers*, XVI, 186.
   The *Gent. Mag.* for Dec. 1793 (LXIII, 1157) lists for 23 Dec.: 'In Boston-row Brompton, in a fit of apoplexy, Rev. Mr. Harrison, late rector of St. John Clerkenwell, minister of Brompton Chapel, and one of the joint preachers of the Magdalen. The merits of Mr. H. are too well known to need an encomium. As a Reader and Preacher, he stood in the foremost rank of popularity; and actually

Notes on the Diary

preached an admirable sermon on the day before his death. As a man he was universally respected. Of the tranquillity of his temper it is sufficient to say that he was a "Complete Angler".'

68   *The Tragedy of Tragedies; or, The Life and Death of Tom Thumb the Great*, by Henry Fielding, and *Chrononhotonthologos, the most Tragical Tragedy that ever was Tragediz'd by any Company of Tragedians*, by Henry Carey, both burlesqued the ranting of much of the serious drama of the day.

69   By Benjamin Hoadly. The *Morning Post* for this day lists the performance at Covent Garden. Included in the cast were Mrs Barry and Mrs Mattocks. The comedy was followed by what was called 'a new pastoral masque and pantomime called The Druids'. This pantomime had been very popular, and on 10 March the *Gazetteer* announced that the 48th performance of the piece would take place the next Monday. The songs had been separately published in 1774.

70   This was the favourite resort of booksellers, and publishers. See Kent, pp. 510–11. For a good account of Coffee House life see W. S. Lewis, *Three Tours through London*, 1941, pp. 32–3.

71   The doors of the theatre opened at 5 o'clock and the performance began at 6.

72   Tragedy by John Hoole. Advertised in the *Morning Post* of 21 March as never performed before at Drury Lane. Miss Younge played the principal female role. 'Gentleman' Smith played Timanthes. Smith had acquired his nick-name 'from his style and tastes, as from his having married a lady of title. His deportment was dignified and manly, his action graceful and never redundant. . . .' (P. Fitzgerald, *New History of the English Stage*, 1882, ii, 292.)

73   *The Irish Widow* had originally been adapted by Garrick from Molière's *Marriage Forcée*, especially for Mrs Barry. See a review in the *Gent. Mag.* xlii (Nov. 1772), 528–32. The author's name was for some time kept secret because of adverse newspaper criticism. Mrs Greville in this performance played the part intended for Mrs Barry. Dodd played the part of Kecksey.

74   Samuel Slingsby was for many years principal dancer at the Opera House in London. From this, and from teaching dancing to the prominent families, he acquired a large fortune, which he later lost in building speculations. See *Gent. Mag.* lxxxi (April 1811), 402.

Notes on the Diary

75　'Caen Dubh Deelish' ('Darling Black Head') was a well-known Irish tune.

76　William Wynne Ryland, engraver to George III. For accounts of him and of the other Irish artists, see *D.N.B.*

77　Daniel and Robert Perreau, celebrated forgers. See the *London Chronicle*, 16–18 March 1775, for an account of the great excitement caused by their apprehension with Mrs Rudd. See also Boswell, *Private Papers*, XI, 76–7, 297–300 and *Thraliana*, p. 123. I have not been able to find out anything about the Perreaus' sister who was married to Dr Jackson.

78　On the morning of 23 March there had appeared an announcement in the *Morning Chronicle* of the entertainments at Ranelagh House. What had evidently appealed to Campbell was not the vocal and instrumental concert advertised to begin at 7 p.m., but the notice that 'Ladies and Gentlemen may walk in the Rotunda Gardens &c. every day, (Sundays excepted) at One Shilling each'. Ranelagh, with numerous improvements and additions, had just reopened on 16 March. (*Morning Chronicle*, 11 March.)

79　A well-known place of public amusement in Dublin. (Raymond.)

80　Almack's Assembly Rooms in King Street, London, were a celebrated gambling resort, etc.

81　Possibly Henry Fombelle, of the India House, who died at Lisbon in 1793, whither he had gone for the recovery of his health. See *Gent. Mag.* LXIII (May 1793), 479.

82　Richard Woodward, Dean of Clogher.

83　Probably Dr John Campbell. See also n. 154.

84　Cockade (?)—as a badge of livery of servants and coachmen.

85　Galeeny or galina—a guinea-fowl. For other descriptions of the splendid dinners at the Thrales', see W. H. Hutton, *Burford Papers*, 1905, p. 49; and *D'Arblay Diary*, etc.

86　See *Life*, II, 290, 509. Also *D'Arblay Diary*, II, 206–7. The title of the work was *Easy Phraseology, for the use of Young Ladies, who intend to learn the colloquial part of the Italian Language*. It was originally written for the use of Queeney Thrale, and had a Preface by Dr Johnson.

Notes on the Diary

87   The agreement between George Robinson the bookseller and Baretti, dated 4 October 1774, stipulated that the author was to receive £25 immediately, £25 when the book was printed, and £25 when it was printed a second time. (*Adam Catalogue*, III, 15.)

88   For a full description of the letters see *Life*, II, 298, 511–13. Numerous amusing accounts of the quarrel had already appeared in the newspapers. The *Morning Post* for 24 January commented: 'The literary dispute between Dr. J— and Mr. M—, it is apprehended will end rather tragical than otherwise; the rigid philosophy of the former has so far forsaken him upon this occasion, that he has actually challenged his Scotch disputant to meet him on a particular mountain in one of the Western Islands, there to decide by pistol shot this momentous affair. The Doctor is in regular training, and fires already without blinking: Mr. M— has accepted the Doctor's challenge, and given Becket orders to make up a half a dozen *cartridges* with the sacred manuscript of his beloved Ossian, as the certain means of carrying *conviction* to the *heart* of the philosophical infidel.' Then on 1 February the same paper continued: 'A certain Mac having sent two long menacing letters to Dr. Johnson, received the following very laconic and pertinent answer: "I am not to be deterred from detecting an imposter, wherever I find him, by the menaces of a ruffian." Dr. Johnson, says a correspondent, is the only man in the world to deal with such a vain, superficial, conceited people as the Scotch; having a firm, manly, and well-informed mind, he only laughs at the torrents of abuse that are daily poured fourth against him.' On 17 March the *Public Advertiser* announced that 'The Dispute between Mr. McPh———n and Dr. J—h—n is very whimsically represented in the Magic Lantern [an exhibition of caricatures held in the Great Room in Panton Street, near the Haymarket] in the Characters of a Scotch Bagpiper and the Cobler of Cripplegate.'

89   Rev. John Warner was celebrated as a popular preacher. As early as 1766 Joseph Cockfield had written of him: 'his Lectures from the pulpit are spirited and fervent, and his manners not less striking' (Nichols, *Illustrations*, V, 759). He built a chapel of his own in Long-Acre, which he later sold to a Dr King. See the account of his death at the age of sixty-four at his house in St John's Square, Clerkenwell. (*Gent. Mag.* LXX (Jan. 1800), 92.)

Notes on the Diary

90   'Ex noto fictum carmen sequar, ut sibi quivis speret idem.'
(Horace, *Ars Poet.* 241.)

91   The *Morning Post* for Monday, 27 March, carried the
advertisement for the evening's entertainment of the Pantheon,
and added that it was to be the last night but one before the Easter
Holidays. The doors were to open at seven o'clock and the concert
would begin at eight. Vocal parts were to be sung by Signora
Agujari, Signora Gallucci, Signor Salvoi, and Mr Meredith. The
orchestra would be under the direction of Mr Giardini. Single
tickets could be purchased for twelve shillings.

The Pantheon, located at No. 173 Oxford Street, had opened in
1772. The next year Horace Walpole wrote that it was 'still the
most beautiful edifice in England' (*Letters*, VIII, 313); but Johnson
had not been much impressed. See *Life*, II, 168–9; and Kent,
499–500.

92   Joachim Karl, Graf von Maltzan was Prussian Minister to
England in 1775.

93   The Duke of Cumberland and Lady Grosvenor had previously had an intrigue.

94   A pagan King in *Orlando Furioso*, whose magic helmet is
acquired by Rinaldo.

95   For descriptions of the absurd head-dresses of the mid-
eighteenth century see George Paston, *Social Caricature in the
Eighteenth Century*, and W. S. Lewis, *Three Tours through London*.
The head-dresses were a constant source of jokes in the newspapers,
e.g. the *Morning Post*, 7 April 1778, the *Public Advertiser*, 8 April
and *Lloyd's Evening Post*, 11 April.

96   Lady Grosvenor was noted for her lax morals. Mrs Thrale,
in December 1778, wrote in her Diary: 'Lady Grosvenor is very
avaricious says somebody; odd enough observed Mrs Cotton—
Women of *that Disposition* are seldom covetous; I see many of
them care no more for Money than the Pope.—Why the Pope is
somewhat a bad Example replies Seward, for he grants *Indulgencies*
for *Money* you know:—so indeed does Lady Grosvenor.'
(*Thraliana*, p. 356.)

97   See L. Collison-Morley, *Giuseppe Baretti*, 1909, p. 280.
Vallancey's *Essay*, etc. had appeared in 1772.

98   For Lord Dacre's interest in antiquities see pp. 16–17.

Notes on the Diary

99   A character in Foote's *The Author*. The man whom Foote was satirising was actually named Apreece. See Mary M. Belden, *The Dramatic Work of Samuel Foote*, 1929, pp. 73-4.

100   Probably William Lennard Roper and Richard Henry Roper, clergymen from county Monaghan, and neighbours of both Campbell and Lord Dacre. They may have been relatives of Lord Dacre (his middle name was Lennard). In any case, he was responsible for making Richard Henry Roper the Rector of Clones. See Shirley's *Monaghan*, pp. 310, 327.

101   See pp. 93-4.

102   Probably an engraving of a head by Ottavio Leoni, an Italian painter and engraver.

103   A play by Arthur Murphy.

104   By Ambrose Philips, from Racine's *Andromaque*. Mrs Canning played Andromache, and was hissed for a bad performance (*Drury Lane Calendar*, ed. MacMillan (1938), p. 186). 'The favourite Tambourine Dance' of Mr Slingsby was listed as 'for that night only'. The tragedy was followed by Garrick's burlesque *A Peep Behind the Curtain, or the New Rehearsal*, with King as Glib and Vernon as Orpheus.

105   *An Answer to a Pamphlet entitled Taxation no Tyranny. Addressed to the Author, and to Persons in Power*. Published anonymously in March 1775.

106   Thrale's house was across the Thames in Southwark, next to his brewery, and not in a fashionable living quarter.

107   For Boswell's attitude towards Baretti see *Life*, I, 302; II, 8, 97; V, 121; *Fettercairn Catalogue*, ed. C. C. Abbott (1936), No. 1039; and Collison-Morley, *Giuseppe Baretti*, pp. 202-24.

108   Johnson that day dined with William Gerard Hamilton to meet Bruce the Abyssinian traveller. Because of a mix-up of plans, Boswell had received a special card of invitation from Thrale to dine with him. (*Private Papers*, x, 170.) Before walking across London Bridge to Southwark, Boswell had spent some time visiting with Johnson.

109   In the *Life* (II, 188, 193) Boswell tells the two parts of the anecdote separately. On 15 April 1772 Boswell defended 'convivial indulgence in wine', although Johnson was not in a very good humour, and had recourse to the maxim, *in vino veritas*.

Notes on the Diary

Johnson replied: 'Why, Sir, that may be an argument for drinking, if you suppose men in general to be liars. But, Sir, I would not keep company with a fellow, who lyes as long as he is sober, and whom you must make drunk before you can get a word of truth out of him.' Then in a general review of the spring of 1772 Boswell adds: 'A gentleman having to some of the usual arguments for drinking added this: "You know, Sir, drinking drives away care, and makes us forget whatever is disagreeable. Would not you allow a man to drink for that reason?" Johnson. "Yes, Sir, if he sat next *you*."' In the Journal (ix, 88) it is all one anecdote.

Mrs Piozzi, in her *Anecdotes* (*John. Misc.* I, 321), tells the first part of the story, with the point somewhat garbled.

110 Cf. *Life*, v, 346. 'Come,' said Johnson, 'let me know what it is that makes a Scotsman happy.' (*Tour to the Hebrides*, ed. Pottle and Bennett, p. 348.)

111 See *Life*, I, 103–5; II, 435; III, 245. Also *Thraliana*, p. 186. Mrs Thrale records: 'With regard to Drink his liking is for the *strongest*, as it is not the Flavour but the Effect of Wine which he even professes to desire, and he used often to pour Cappillaire into his glass of Port when it was his Custom to drink Wine which he has now left wholly off.'

112 *Life*, II, 330; *Private Papers*, x, 171. It was that morning at Johnson's house that the conversation had occurred. The solution to the mystery is probably found in one of Johnson's early letters to Miss Boothby (*Letters*, I, 49) where he describes the use of powdered orange peel as a cure for indigestion.

113 *Life*, v, 138.

114 In his Journal Boswell also records these remarks, though not in so much detail as Campbell. See *Private Papers*, x, 173. The fact that Boswell tells the two anecdotes in reverse sequence need not discredit Campbell's order, for Boswell two weeks later admitted that 'When I put down Mr. Johnson's sayings, I do not keep strictly to Chronology.' It cannot be stressed too strongly that the agreement of Campbell and Boswell about the conversation does not prove in any way that Johnson actually used the words here recorded. Neither ever heard Johnson use language which might be considered bawdy. On the other hand, it is perfectly possible that in his earlier days, when in rough bachelor company, Johnson did on occasions use language which he would have

Notes on the Diary

strictly avoided in later years. What we have here, then, is merely second or third hand gossip about something which occurred long before, and it cannot be considered trustworthy evidence. The answer to the question 'What is the greatest pleasure?' is told by Murphy, who was not noted for accuracy (see n. 118), on the authority of Garrick, who was not present. The other episode, according to Boswell, was vouched for by both Murphy and Thrale, and thus may be more authentic. The conclusion of this anecdote is differently told by Boswell. He merely adds, instead of 'Damn the rascal, etc.' the sentence 'Was not this a gross fellow?'

Dr James had been one of Johnson's early acquaintances. See A.L. Reade, *op. cit.*, III, 124; *Thraliana*, p. 173.

115   *Life*, v, 54. 'Ay,' said Dr Johnson, 'that is the state of the world. Water is the same everywhere. Una est injusti caerula forma maris.'

116   The meaning of this passage is not clear. Perhaps Campbell misunderstood Murphy, who, we know, had studied Greek in his youth. (He had once made a translation—never printed—of Euripides' *Iphigenia*, presumably from the Greek.) Murphy would certainly have recognised the quoted Greek tag as a frequent beginning of a Homeric line, bearing no relation to the transliterated Greek from Epictetus which occurs in chapter xxv of the *Vicar of Wakefield*. What possibly happened was this: Murphy said that Goldsmith in the *Vicar of Wakefield* had ridiculed the moral standard of a fitness of things better than Fielding in *Tom Jones*. Where? In the person of the villain who in prison and elsewhere supports his opinion by quoting sentences from Epictetus. But Goldsmith probably took the device of quoting Greek from Fielding, witness the scene in *Joseph Andrews* where the village surgeon pretends to know Greek and quotes from Homer the common tag *Ton dapomibominos....* Campbell missed, or perhaps did not hear, the transition.

117   Campbell had seen the play on 4 March. See pp. 44–5.

118   In his Journal Boswell thus records this incident (x, 172): 'Murphy again told his story of a Scotsman's introduction to Mr. Johnson, *Come from Scotland*, etc., as if he had been present. "Why," said Baretti, "it was Mr. Boswell." Murphy tried to escape by saying that I was not then of such consequence as to make

him remember that I was the person. I could not resist any longer correcting his inaccuracy, and told him he was *not present*. "You are confounding what you have *heard* with what you have *seen*," said I.'

119   Possibly the first two commandments. (Raymond.) John Moore was then Bishop of Bangor.

120   Richard Terrick.

121   Whether authentic or not, this story is still told in modern guide books, etc. See Kent, p. 204.

122   In this instance Campbell's memory played him false. Mr E. G. Millar writes that both copies of the Magna Carta in the British Museum formed part of the Cottonian Library.

123   In the MS. there is a crude sketch of the pulpit.

124   The *London Chronicle* for 4 April has an account of the proceedings, so long depending in the Court of Chancery. It was an appeal from an order of the Lord Chancellor; the appellants were the present Duke and Duchess of Montagu, the Duke of Buccleuch and his wife and their eldest son; the respondents were Lord Beaulieu, and Lady Beaulieu, late Duchess Dowager of Manchester. The *Morning Chronicle* for 5 April gives an account of the speakers the day before, including Lord Camden, Lord Mansfield, Lord Abercorn, and the Lord Chancellor.

125   In Boswell's account of the day (x, 187–8) he tells of walking across London Bridge for a chat with Mrs Thrale (see p. 2), then to Westminister and down the river in a boat. 'I landed at the Temple, took up Campbell at the Grecian Coffee-house, and he and I walked to Dilly's.'

126   Afterwards Sir John Miller of Batheaston, husband of Lady Anna Miller, the traveller and Blue-Stocking. Boswell this day recorded of Miller that he appeared 'much better than I expected; for I expected to see a mere Frible, and found him a tall, well looking man, very elegantly drest, and, though a coxcomb, not so trifling as I imagined.'

127   John Scott of Amwell, a Quaker poet, who had recently published some elegies. See *Life*, ii, 338, 351. Bennet Langton was also a member of the company.

Notes on the Diary

128   For a list of the various attacks on *Taxation No Tyranny*, see Courtney-Nichol Smith, *Bibliography of Johnson*, pp. 125–7. Many of these were reviewed in the *Monthly Review*, LII (May, 1775), 446–50.

129   *Monthly Review*, LII (March 1775), 253–61. The review was written by Griffiths.

130   See *Life*, III, 39 (12 April 1776), where Boswell records asking a question 'with an assumed air of ignorance, to incite him to talk, for which it was often necessary to employ some address'. The Provincial Assemblies referred to were those of the thirteen American colonies.

131   Johnson once told Sir Joshua Reynolds that on one occasion 'when he dined in a numerous company of booksellers, where the room being small, the head of the table, at which he sat, was almost close to the fire, he persevered in suffering a great deal of inconvenience from the heat, rather than quit his place, and let one of them sit above him'. (*Life*, III, 311.)

132   As he noted in his Journal, Boswell left at seven o'clock, because of a business engagement (x, 189).

133   George Buchanan, who died in 1582.

134   On 30 April 1773, Johnson said to Boswell: 'I have not read Hume; but, doubtless, Goldsmith's History is better than the *verbiage* of Robertson.' (*Life*, II, 236.)

135   Dr Robert Lowth, Bishop of Oxford. His work here referred to was *Praelectiones de Sacra Poesi Hebraeorum*.

136   James Ussher, Archbishop of Armagh, who died in 1656. Johnson had previously spoken of him to Maxwell as the 'great luminary of the Irish church'. (*Life*, II, 132.)

137   Johnson wrote of Congreve: 'Southern mentioned him with sharp censure, as a man that meanly disowned his native country'; and of Swift: 'he was contented to be called an Irishman by the Irish, but would occasionally call himself an Englishman.' (*Lives of the Poets*, II, 212; III, 1.) But the most recent biographer of Congreve proves conclusively that Congreve was born in Yorkshire, and did not go to Ireland until he was four years old. (J. C. Hodges, *William Congreve the Man*, 1941, pp. 5–8.)

Notes on the Diary

138 In the spring of 1777, when writing to Charles O'Connor in Ireland (see pp. 12–13), Johnson refers to Ireland as once the 'school of the west, the quiet habitation of sanctity and literature' (*Life*, III, 112). On 1 May 1773 Johnson remarked to Boswell: 'The Irish mix better with the English than the Scotch do...they have not that extreme nationality which we find in the Scotch' (*Life*, II, 242).

139 The *Morning Post* for 6 April has an account of the proceedings. Campbell, as a political conservative, was irritated by Allen's speech, but the *Lloyd's Evening Post* for 5–7 April calls it 'long and eloquent', and quotes liberally from it. 'The Americans', he said, 'are sons of Britons, and have a Right to be free.' Campbell's reactions to such remarks are symptomatic of his political beliefs, even though at another time he was shocked by Johnson's anger at the colonists. (See p. 95.)

140 This remark obviously refers to something Johnson said at dinner. Boswell's version points the anecdote at Isaac Hawkins Browne: 'We talked of speaking in Publick. Mr. Johnson said that one of the first wits of this Country, Isaac Hawkins Brown, got into Parliament and never opened his mouth. Mr. Johnson said that it was more disgraceful not to try to speak than to try and fail, as it was more disgraceful not to fight than to fight and be beat....' (*Private Papers*, X, 188.) It is possible that both Boswell and Campbell are right and that Johnson mentioned Addison as well as Browne as examples of timidity in speaking.

141 This was a letter from Swift to Dr Jenny of Armagh. Writing to Bishop Percy on 21 March 1809 (*The Correspondence of Thomas Percy and Edmond Malone*, ed. Arthur Tillotson, 1944, pp. 246–7) Malone states that he procured the letter for John Nichols. Nichols, in a footnote on p. 171 of J. Barrett's *Essay on the Earlier Part of the Life of Swift*, 1808, writes: "this perfectly characteristic Letter, which has been among the *desiderata* of all former editions, is now first printed by the favour of Lord Viscount Cremorne, in whose family it has been preserved. The letter had been many years ago noticed by Dr Thomas Campbell, an Irish clergyman, in his 'Philosophical Survey of the South of Ireland.'" In fact Lord Dartry (later Viscount Cremorne) did not print it in 1775, though he promised Campbell that he would. F. Elrington Ball prints the letter in his edition of Swift's *Correspondence*, 1910–14, IV, 303–6, taking his text from Barrett's *Essay*.

Notes on the Diary

142   The opera, as advertised by the *Morning Post*, etc., was Niccola Piccinni's *La Buona Figliuola*, based on a libretto by Goldoni. It was first performed at the Haymarket on 9 December 1766. The principal singers in 1775 were Signors Lovattini and Fochetti; and Signoras Galli, Farinella, Spilletta and Sestini.

143   Another guest was a Mr Gillon, nephew of Gillon of Walhouse's, who had been to Guadaloupe, and had sent Thrale the fine liqueurs, which Boswell enjoyed. (*Private Papers*, x, 199.)

144   Boswell lists Lady Elizabeth Cosby Fitzroy as one of the guests (*Private Papers*, x, 199). Elizabeth Jeffries was her daughter by a second husband, James Jeffries (see *Gent. Mag.* LXXII (1802, pt. 1), 94). General Sir John Irwin was another member of the party.

145   Northcote describes her as 'the Grosvenor Square of Comedy' (*Conversations of Northcote*, p. 298). And Garrick once referred to her as 'that worst of bad women' (*Correspondence*, II, 141). Yet Johnson was flattered and pleased by her attentions. See *Life*, II, 330, and *Letters*, I, 316.

146   See also *Life*, II, 77. An amusing anecdote about Johnson and the Scotch—how accurate it is impossible to estimate—was printed in the *London Chronicle* for 29 April–2 May: 'A Gentleman the other day, in conversation with Dr. J——n, was very gravely expressing his amazement that the Doctor should entertain so much hatred and aversion to the Scots, who had treated him so civilly in his late tour amongst them; when he received the following short reply: "Sir, you are exceedingly misinformed with respect to this matter; I do not *hate* the Scots: Sir, I do not *hate* frogs, in the water, though I confess I do not like to have them hopping about my bedchamber."'

147   In his Journal for Good Friday, 14 April, Boswell wrote: 'I told him that Mr. Orme said many parts of the East Indies were better mapped than the highlands of Scotland. Said Mr. Johnson: "That a country may be mapped, it must be travelled over." "Nay," said I, "can't you say it is not *worth* mapping?"' The similarity of this account to that recorded by Campbell would lead one to suspect that they represent different versions of the same remarks. Moreover, since Boswell noted on 27 April that he was writing up his Journal for most of the month 'from imperfect notes a good while after the days have past;' (x, 189) and since just before telling the above anecdote Boswell admitted that he

was not keeping to strict chronology in putting down Johnson's sayings, we may be safe in suspecting that the conversation occurred as Campbell has it on the 8th. Another bit of evidence bearing on the question is the fact that Boswell had met Orme at a Ball at the Mansion House the night of 7 April. He would naturally have told Johnson of Orme's remarks at the first opportunity, which would have been at Thrale's the next day.

148 See *Life*, III, 100; and K. Balderston, *History and Sources of Percy's Memoir of Goldsmith*, 1926.

149 For William Kenrick, see *D.N.B.* and *Life*, I, 497–8.

150 *Life*, III, 70, 312; *D'Arblay Diary*, I, 58.

151 Boswell's version is substantially the same: 'Mrs. Thrale told us that Mr. Johnson had said that Barry was just fit to stand at the door of an Auction-room with a long pole: "Pray, Gentlemen, walk in." She said Murphy said Garrick was fit for that, and would pick your pocket after you came out. Mr. Johnson said there was no wit there. "You may say of any man that he will pick a pocket. Besides, the man at the door does not pick pockets. That is to be done within, by the Auctioneer."' (*Private Papers*, x, 199.)

Garrick was reputed to be very careful of his own money. Mrs Piozzi later wrote down a possibly apocryphal story in her Commonplace Book that Foote placed a bust of Garrick upon his escritoire. 'There, (says he) you Dog, take Care of my Money— as you take Care of your own, *do.*' 'If he is so sharp,' replies Murphy, 'methinks, you should not trust him on your Bureau.' 'Oh,' answers Foote, 'He has no Hands you see.'

152 This was Swift's favourite expression.

153 The Rev. John Burrows held the living of St Clement Danes from 1773 until his death in 1786. For a full account of him see Montague Burrows, *History of the Family of Burrows*, 1877, pp. 33 ff. See also *Life*, III, 379, 531; R. Blunt, *Mrs Montagu Queen of the Blues*; and the *D'Arblay Diary*.

154 Dr John Campbell. The year before he had published a *Political Survey of Great Britain*, which may have given Campbell some ideas for his own first book. Sir John Hawkins, in his *Life of Johnson*, pp. 210–11, states: 'His residence for some years before his death, was the large new-built house situate at the north-west corner of Queen square, Bloomsbury, whither, parti-

cularly on a Sunday evening, great numbers of persons of the first eminence for science and literature were accustomed to resort for the enjoyment of conversation.' Johnson once remarked to Boswell, 'I used to go pretty often to Campbell's on a Sunday evening, till I began to consider that the shoals of Scotchman who flocked about him might probably say, when any thing of mine was well done, "Ay, ay, he has learnt this of CAWMELL".' (*Life*, I, 418.)

155　See A.A. Ettinger, *James Edward Oglethorpe*, 1936, pp. 302–3. It was Boswell who took Campbell to Oglethorpe's.

156　See *Life*, I, 127–8; II, 180–1. Pope's *Imitations of Horace*, II, 2, 276.

157　Boswell wrote in his Journal: 'We had a good dinner and Sicilian wine as usual....He [Johnson] pressed General Oglethorpe to give his life, saying, "I know no man alive whose life would be—." The General seemed very unwilling to enter upon it.' In the *Life* (II, 350), Boswell warns the reader not to suppose that his record 'contains the whole of what was said by Johnson...'. For this day Campbell's account is much fuller than Boswell's.

158　The London newspapers, perhaps as a joke, did announce that Johnson had been burned in effigy in America. The *St James's Chronicle* for 10–13 June 1775, carried the report: 'The last Advices from *Boston* (among other Particulars equally curious) bring Word that on the Arrival of *Taxation No Tyranny*, a celebrated political Pamphlet, the supposed author of it was burnt in Effigy at *Salem*. He was first carried through the Streets, preceded by a Number of Musicians who played the noted Tune of *Yanky Doodle*, that very tune which so charmed the truly musical Ears of the late Mr *Joel Collier*, when he heard it performed on the Banks of the *Severn*. The Head of the Figure was decorated with a Perriwig which is said to have been purchased from *James Boswell*, Esq., who designed to have kept it as a Relick of his Saint; but, with a Spirit truly *Corsican*, consented to part with it on the Supposition that it might serve the Cause of Liberty which its ancient Master had deserted. The Cloaths in which this Representative of the Pensioner appeared, consisted of a Suit resembling that in which he so gracefully returned Thanks to *Lord Bute* for his Patronage. We have no Doubt (says our *Boston* Correspondent) if he should write a second Pamphlet, to prove

Notes on the Diary

that the Troops of *General Gage* did *not* run away from the Provincials, and that *Lord Percy* has *only* ravished the Wives of Messrs. *Hancock* and *Otis* but that the Doctor will at the same Time take an Opportunity to return us Sesquipedalian Thanks for the Honour we have conferred upon him.' (First reprinted in the *Johnsonian News Letter* for June 1941.)

159 According to Boswell, on 21 March Johnson had 'persevered in his wild allegation, that he questioned if there was a tree between Edinburgh and the English border older than himself.' (*Life*, II, 311.) Although there is no evidence that Johnson was ever hanged in effigy in Scotland, the possibility was at least suggested in an amusingly satirical letter from a reader in Edinburgh, published in the *Morning Post* for 30 January.

160 Probably *The Graces; a Poetical Epistle from a Gentleman to his Son*, which appeared in 1775 (London, Flexney, 4to). The *London Chronicle* for 16–18 Feb. attributes it to William Woty.

161 See *Life*, IV, 79, 80; *John. Misc.* I, 212.

162 Johnson had said the same thing at Thrale's on 28 March. 'No, Sir,' said he. 'There are but two good Stanzas in Gray's Poetry, in his *Church yard*.' (*Private Papers*, x, 159.) Possibly it was Boswell's insistence on getting him to repeat observations made only shortly before that irritated Johnson.

163 Boswell ended his account of the conversation by admitting: 'He was not in the humour of talking, and I tried several times to set him agoing, which displeased him; for Langton told me he said when they were in the coach, "When Boswell gets wine, his conversation consists all of questions."' (*Private Papers*, x, 204.) 'Questioning', said Johnson on another occasion, 'is not the mode of conversation among gentlemen.' (*Life*, II, 472.) See also *Life*, III, 57, 268.

164 When in the Hebrides with Boswell, Johnson gave a similar opinion. Boswell suggested the case of a man who knows that in a few days he will be detected of a fraud, which will entail disgrace and expulsion from society. Johnson replied: 'Then, sir, let him go abroad to a distant country; let him go to some place where he is *not* known. Don't let him go to the devil where he *is* known!' (*Tour to the Hebrides*, ed. Pottle and Bennett, p. 35.) See also *Private Papers*, VI, 146 (facsimile).

Notes on the Diary

165   The reading is not clear. Raymond transcribed the name as Wilkinson, but I suspect it may be Watkinson, the man to whom Campbell directed the letters in his *Philosophical Survey*.

166   Rampiked—decaying or dead, as of a stump.

167   Possibly Thomas Mosse who had been a student at Trinity College, Dublin, with Campbell. Mosse entered in 1753 and received his B.A. in the spring of 1757, a year later than Campbell.

168   The *Morning Chronicle* for 13 April announced: 'This day his Majesty will go to the House of Peers and give the Royal Assent to the Bill for restraining the trade of the Colonies of New Jersey, Pensylvania &c., the American Mutiny bill, the Indemnity bill, the bill for appointing Commissioners to the Land-Tax, and to several other public and private bills.' The next morning the papers described the King's going in state. See also *Annual Register*, 1775, p. 107.

169   The Rev. William Dodd who was executed for forgery in 1777. See *Gent. Mag.* xlvii (1777), 92, 115, 339, 421; *Life*, iii, 139–48.

170   'For if we have been planted together in the likeness of his death, we shall be also in the likeness of his resurrection.'

171   Richard Robinson, Archbishop of Armagh, and first Lord Rokeby. He was the cousin of Mrs Elizabeth Montagu, 'Queen of the Blue-Stockings'. W. Childe-Pemberton, in *The Earl Bishop*, 1924, p. 357, calls him 'a man of narrow outlook and little perspicuity'.

172   In the Tower of London.

173   Dr Alexander Bissett, Chancellor of Armagh, and Archdeacon of Connor. (J.B. Leslie, *Armagh Clergy*, p. 39.)

174   It is not clear which Scott is here referred to.

175   Marcus Paterson, Chief Justice of the Common Pleas in Ireland. (He died 1787.) The slow advancement in the church of his brother William was a matter of much concern to Dr Campbell. William was no ascetic churchman, and once on his way to church thrashed a man whom he saw beating his wife. (H.B. Swanzy, *The Vicars of Newry*, pp. 15–20.)

176   Unfortunately, Boswell was away from London from 19 April to 2 May, so that we have no more opportunities to compare his records of Johnson's conversation with those of Campbell.

Notes on the Diary

177   The Rev. Nathan Wetherell, Master of University College, Oxford. He told Boswell on 14 April that he had been largely responsible for securing Johnson's Doctor's Degree from Oxford. (*Private Papers*, x, 214.) On this trip to London, Wetherell appears to have been seeking preferment for himself, for the *Morning Post* for 27 April announced that 'Yesterday the Rev. Doctor Wetherell kissed his Majesty's hand at St. James's, on his promotion to the Canonry of the Collegiate Church of St. Peter's Westminster.' For the attempt to set up a riding academy at Oxford with Carter as Master, see *Thraliana*, pp. 116–19; and Johnson's *Letters*, i, 309, 312–13, 323, 327, 338, etc.

178   The *Morning Post* for 19 April announced as that day first published *Resistance No Rebellion—in answer to Dr. Johnson's 'Taxation No Tyranny'*. Printed for J. Bell of the Strand, it sold for one shilling. See also n. 128.

179   Johnson always felt very bitter about the American Revolution. See *Life*, iii, 290; ii, 312; *Queeney Letters*, p. 255; and his later remarks to Campbell, pp. 95–6.

180   *Life*, ii, 313, 515.

181   Mr Weld of Clements' Inn I have been unable to identify further.

182   See E.B. Chancellor, *The Private Palaces of London*, 1908, pp. 207–20; Kent, p. 382, etc.

183   An uninvited guest, brought by one who has been invited. Used in this sense by Horace, etc.

184   A crude sketch of the lay-out of the gardens at Hampton Court. See Plate 30 in R.J. Allen's *Life in Eighteenth Century England*, 1941.

185   In February, 1773, Boswell had presented Johnson with an 'elegant Pindar'. Perhaps this was the same volume. (*Life*, ii, 204–5.)

186   For some of Johnson's views about Ireland see *Life*, ii, 121, 130, 255, etc.

187   The Rev. Philip Skelton. In a time of scarcity he once sold his library to supply his poor parishioners with food. His *Ophiomaches, or Deism Revealed*, was published in 1748.

Notes on the Diary

188   Patrick Delany, the friend of Swift. See *Life*, III, 249–50.

189   Robert Clayton, Bishop of Clogher, who died in 1758. In 1751 he had published an *Essay* full of Arian doctrine, which led to a long controversy. Finally he was prosecuted for heresy, but before the appointed time of the trial he was seized with a nervous disorder and died. (*D.N.B.*)

190   James Portis, a stockbroker. See *N. and Q.* 10 Feb. 1945.

191   The sixteenth annual exhibition of the Incorporated Society of Artists of Great Britain, held at their rooms near Exeter-Exchange in the Strand, was opened 25 April. See *Daily Advertiser* for 24 April.

192   The *British Chronicle* for 26 April: 'Yesterday the exhibition of Pictures, Statues, &c. was opened, for the seventh time, at the Royal Academicians' Great Room in Pall Mall. The articles which seemed most to engage the attention of the public were, Landscapes and Cattle by Messrs. Barrett, Crone, Dall, Tompkins, and Wilson; the death of Adonis by Barry; Fish and Birds, by Elmer; Sappho, the despair of Achilles, and the return of Telemachus, by Mrs. Kaufman. . . .'

193   The Grand Masked Ball at the Pantheon, advertised in the *Morning Chronicle* for 27 April as the only one that season, was attended by about 900 masqueraders. (*London Chronicle*, 29 April.) The doors opened at 9.30, supper was at 12, and the tickets were two guineas each.

194   *Lloyd's Evening Post* described the excessive heat which kept down the attendance at the masquerade, and added: 'At about four o'clock the champaigne operated so far as to cause a great deal of noise; but no disputes or disturbance; the company were not all departed at seven in the morning.'

195   Speene or Speenhamland, the Roman Spinae, adjoins or rather forms part of the town of Newbury. (Raymond.)

196   Pope's 3rd Moral Essay, To Lord Bathurst, 'On the Use of Riches', line 307.

197   Daughter of the Duke of Grafton by his first wife.

198   Charles, Viscount Mahon, afterwards 3rd Earl Stanhope, married Lady Hester Pitt.

199   It has not proved possible to identify accurately many of the people at Bath mentioned by Campbell.

Notes on the Diary

200 Possibly the Rev. Thomas Goddard, vicar of South Petherton, and Clevedon, county Somerset, and minister of Barrow in the same county. He died in 1789. (*Gent. Mag.* LIX (Aug. 1789), 768.)

201 Droitwich. (Raymond.)

202 Since Baskerville had only recently died (8 January 1775), his life and eccentricities were probably still much talked about in his home community. He had been noted for his disbelief in Christianity. Indeed, John Wilkes, himself something of a sceptic, once said of Baskerville, 'he was a terrible infidel; he used to shock me'. (*N. and Q.*, 1st series, VIII, 203.) For details of his life see R. Straus and R.K. Dent, *John Baskerville.*

203 It was by this nephew that Campbell's *Diary* later was taken to New South Wales. See pp. xii, xiii, 14.

204 Campbell printed this conversation in his *Strictures* in 1789 (p. 336). See pp. 14, 23. For a comparison of the two versions see *John. Misc.* II, 56–7.

205 Cf. *Life*, II, 255.

206 The Rev. Dr Maxwell of Falkland in Ireland told Boswell that Johnson once 'severely reprobated the barbarous debilitating policy of the British government, which, he said, was the most detestable mode of persecution. To a gentleman, who hinted such policy might be necessary to support the authority of the English government, he replied by saying, "Let the authority of the English government perish, rather than be maintained by iniquity. Better would it be to restrain the turbulence of the natives by the authority of the sword..."'. (*Life*, II, 121.)

207 See *Life*, III, 205; *Letters*, I, 107.

208 See pp. 23–5.

209 Grimr Johnson Thorkelin, Keeper of the Archives at Copenhagen. He studied the MS. of Beowulf in London in 1787 and in 1815 produced the first edition of the poem.

210 See n. 1, p. 27.

211 It is interesting to compare Campbell's reactions to various places in Paris with those of Johnson and Mrs Thrale in 1775. See *The French Journals of Mrs Thrale and Doctor Johnson*, ed. Tyson and Guppy, 1932.

Notes on the Diary

212   'Haec placuit semel, haec deciens repetita placebit.' (Horace, *Ars Poet.* 365.)

213   Probably the Rev. Edward Blakeway (1736/37–1795). See Nichols' *Illustrations*, v, 643.

214   Possibly a brother of Mrs Fitzherbert, and one of the four sons of Walter Smythe, second son of Sir John Smythe, 3rd baronet. The Smythes were a well-known Catholic family. (L. Bettany, *Edward Jerningham and His Friends*, 1919, p. 26.)

215   William Sturgeon, married to Lady Henrietta Alicia Wentworth. See Horace Walpole's letter to the Earl of Hertford, 1 Nov. 1764. In another place he calls her Harriet.

216   William Henry Fortescue, Earl of Clermont, of Clermont in the County of Louth. In 1789 he was appointed a gentleman of the bed-chamber to the Prince of Wales. (*Gent. Mag.* XLVII (Jan. 1777), 48; LIX (Supplement 1789), 1215.)

217   Charles, 2nd Viscount Maynard. (*Gent. Mag.* XLV (July 1775), 351.) Walpole, in a letter to Mann, 29 Jan. 1779, calls him 'the poor simple Maynard'. He had married the well-known Nancy Parsons who had been kept by the Dukes of Grafton, Dorset, etc.

218   See pp. 28–30.

219   Rev. William Kirwan, later Dean of Killala, and a celebrated preacher in Dublin. An excellent account of his great talents as a speaker and the universal mourning at his death may be found in *Gent. Mag.* LXXV (Nov. 1805), 1080–1. For a description of his pulpit oratory see E. Oe. Somerville and M. Ross, *An Incorruptible Irishman*, 1932, pp. 24–5. 'Kirwan's manner of preaching was of the French School. He was vehement for a while, and becoming, or affecting to become, exhausted, he held his handkerchief to his face. A dead silence ensued. He had skill to perceive the precise moment to recommence. Another blaze of declamation burst upon the congregation, and another fit of exhaustion was succeeded by another pause....' (Taken from J. Barrington, *Personal Sketches*.)

220   John Fane, 10th Earl of Westmorland, was Lord Lieutenant of Ireland at this time.

INDEX

139

Index

Bruce, James, African explorer, 1, 124

Buccleuch, Henry Scott, third Duke of, 127

Buchanan, George, Scotch historian, 74, 128

La Buona Figliuola, by Niccola Piccinni, 130

Burke, Edmund, 31, 55, 116; Campbell indebted to, 20, 23; Junius, thought to be, 54, 118; parliament, called to order in, 49, 115

Burke, Richard, 54, 118

Burke, Thomas, engraver, 59

Burlington, Richard Boyle, third Earl of, 71

Burroughs, Rev. Henry, 114

Burrows, Rev. John, 78, 131

Bute, John Stuart, third Earl of, 115, 132

Cadell, Thomas, publisher, 10, 115

Calais, 18, 99

Camden, Charles Pratt, first Earl of, 72, 127

Camden, William, *Britannia*, 16, 18, 23

Campbell, Rev. Charles, xii–xiii, 3

Campbell, Elizabeth Johnston, 2

Campbell, Dr John, 60, 78, 121, 131

Campbell, John Thomas, x–xiii, 14, 94, 137

Campbell, Rev. Moses, 2

Campbell, Dr Thomas

Life: description of, 1–2; birth, 2; education, 2–4; marriage (?), 3–4; church career, 3–4, 13, 99; charity sermons, 13, 16, 22, 31, 32; journeys—to England (1775), 4–7, 35–93, through Southern Ireland (1775), 7–10, to England (1776–7), 10–13, 93, to England (1781), 14, 94–6, to England (1786), 17, 96–9,

expense account, 97–8, to France (1787), 18–20, 99–106, to England (1789–90), 24, 106, to England (1792), 29–30, 106–7; church building in townland Shanco, 27, 28, 99; guardianship of nephew, 28; last years, 30–3; death, 33

Works: Britannia, contributions to, 16–23; *Diary*, character of, ix, x, xv, 4–5, 19, history of, ix–xiv, 14, 137; *Discourse in St Luke's Church, Gallown*, 31–2; *First Lines of Ireland's Interest*, 13; 'History of the Revolutions of Ireland', 13, 17, 20, 31, 34, 96–7, 99; 'Jerneus' sketch, 21, 23; *Letter to the Duke of Portland*, 15; Memoir of Goldsmith, 25–30, 106–7; *Philosophical Survey of the South of Ireland*, ix, 7–12, 15, 20, 21, 22, 93, 129, 134; *A Remedy for the Distilleries of Ireland*, 15; *Sermon preached in St Andrew's Church, Dublin*, 13–14; 'Sketch of the Constitution of Ireland', xv, 22; *Strictures on the Ecclesiastical and Literary History of Ireland*, xv, 14, 23–6, 34, 137

Comments and Opinions: actors, 5, 44–5, 51–2, 59, 66; architecture, 27, 63, 71, 91, 100–1, etc.; business affairs, 10, 15, 51, 102; church procedure, 70, 72, 81, 101; dinners, 61, 64; English character, 44–5, 56, 58, 59, 60, 65, 82–3, 91–2; English and French people, 103–6; Grand Opera, 75; Irish affairs, 7, 9, 10, 13, 30–3, 94–6; Irish antiquity, 74, etc.; Irish, Scotch, and English climates, 93–4; land-

140

Index

Index

Index

Index

Johnson, *Opinions (cont.)*
making, 77; drinking, 68, 124–5; Foster's sermons, 54, 118; Goldsmith, 77; Gray's poetry, 79, 133; the greatest pleasure, 68; Irish antiquity, 13, 17, 74, 129; Irish clerics, 85, 86; Irish politics, xvi, 14, 94–6, 135, 137; Junius, authorship of, 54; The Pantheon, 123; the sea, 69, 126; the Scotch, 73–4, 76, 118, 129, 130, 131, 132–3; Scotland, England, and Ireland compared, 73–4, 129; suicide, 79–80, 133

Works: Baretti's *Easy Phraseology*, preface to, 121; Goldsmith, epitaph on, 11; *Journey to the Western Islands*, 7, 54, 70, 115; *The Patriot*, 70; *Taxation No Tyranny*, 49, 54, 66–7, 70, 72–3, 83–4, 124, 128, 132, 135

Johnston, Baptist, 2
Johnston, George, 2
Jowett, Benjamin, xiii, xv
Judas Macabaeus, oratorio by Handel, 48–9, 114
Junius, 54, 116, 118

K. T., 25

Kelly, Hugh, dramatist, 43, 87, 111
Kenrick, William, 77, 117, 131
Kensington, 80
Kerr, Mrs, 107
Kew Bridge, Surrey, 82
Killeevan church, Monaghan, 4, 18, 27, 33, 93
King John's Palace, Kent, 76
King, Thomas, actor, 51–2, 65, 124
Kirwan, Rev. William, 107, 138
Kneller, Sir Godfrey, painter, 84–5
Knowles, 'Widow', 93

Lambal, Marie-Thérèse-Louise de Savoie-Carignan, Princesse de, 102
Langton, Bennet, 79, 127, 133
Langton, William, Dean of Clogher, 89
Larman, Mr, 89
Le Brun, Charles, painter, 85
Ledwich, Rev. Edward, 21, 25, 34
Leeson, Ida E., librarian of Mitchell Library, Sydney, xiv
Leinster, James FitzGerald, first Duke of, 55
Leoni, Ottavio, artist, 65, 124
Lisson, Mr, 55
Livy (Titus Livius), historian, 6
London, Richard Terrick, Bishop of, 70, 127
Louis XIV, King of France, 101–2
Louis (-Stanislas-Xavier) XVIII, 101
Louth (or Lowth), Robert, Bishop of Oxford, 74, 128
Luttrell, Lady Elizabeth, 89
Lyttelton, George, first Baron, 117–18
Lyttelton, Thomas, second Baron, 63

MacArdell, James, engraver, 59
Macaulay, Thomas Babington, x–xvi
MacKenzie, Miss, 89
Macpherson, James, *History of Great Britain*, 49, 115; letters to and from Johnson, 61, 122; *Ossian*, 9, 12, 61, 115, 122
MacQuarie, General Lachlan, x, xii
Madden, William John, 89
Magic Lantern, Panton St, 122
Magna Carta, 71, 127
Mahon, Charles Stanhope, Viscount, 89, 136
Mahon, Lady Hester (Pitt), 89, 136

144

Index

Index

Index

Southerne, Thomas, dramatist, 74, 128

Sparks, Mrs, Irish actress, 59

Speenhamland, Berks, 87, 136

Spring Gardens, Bath, 88

Stanley, John, musician, 48, 114

Steele, Sir Richard, 10, 111

Stormont, David Murray, seventh Viscount, 63

Strahan, William, printer, 10–11, 115

Stratford on Avon, 8, 40–1

Strathmore, Mary Eleanor (Bowes), Countess of (?), 98

Sturgeon, William, 102, 138

Sturz, Helferich Peter, 116

The Suspicious Husband, by Benjamin Hoadly, 58, 120

Swanzy, Henry, Dean of Dromore, 4

Swift, Jonathan, 74, 75, 128, 129, 131; *Gulliver's Travels*, 45–6, 113

Taxation Tyranny, 72

Taylor, Rev. John, 119

Thompson, Sir C., 76

Thompson's inn, St Asaph, 39

Thorkelin, Grimr Johnson, 17, 97, 137

Thrale, Henry, 5, 51, 53, 54, 55, 60, 61, 64, 67, 68, 76, 83, 116, 124, 130

Thrale, Mrs Hester Lynch (Salusbury), 61, 67, 70, 77, 119, 127; Baretti flatters, 53; characterizes Campbell, xi, 1, 2; described by Campbell, 51, by Sturz, 116; her health in 1776–7, 10; meets Campbell in 1792, 29; her Commonplace Book, 131; *Thraliana*, 10, 123, 125

Thrale, Hester Maria, 1, 121

Thurlow, Edward, first Baron, 45

Thurlow, Dr Thomas, 45, 113

Timanthes, by John Hoole, 58–9, 119–20

Tower of London, 55–6, 81, 134

Townshend, Anne (Montgomery), Viscountess, 64

Townshend, George, fourth Viscount, 46–7, 113

Trinity College, Dublin, 3, 12, 53, 117

Ussher, James, Archbishop of Armagh, 74, 128

Vallancey, Charles, antiquary, 8, 20, 23, 24, 25, 64, 96, 106, 123

van Loo, Charles-André (?), painter, 59

Vauxhall Gardens, 103

Vernon, Joseph, actor, 44, 112, 124

Versailles, 101–2, 103, 104

Vesuvius, 72

Vincent, Mr, musician, 114

Viny, John, wheelwright, 50, 116

The Virginians, novel by Thackeray, xi

Voltaire, François-Marie Arouet de, 12, 113

Walker, Joseph Cooper, 21, 22, 34

Waller, Miss, 89

Walpole, Horace, 123

Warner, Rev. John, 62, 122

Watkinson, John, M.D., 7, 11, 14, 134

Watson, James, engraver, 59

Waugh and Cox, Sydney booksellers, ix

Welch, Daniel Lovett, Sydney printer, ix

Weld, Mr, 84, 87, 135

Wentworth, Lady Henrietta Alicia, 102, 138

Index